Thomas Mann

Titles in the series Critical Lives present the work of leading cultural figures of the modern period. Each book explores the life of the artist, writer, philosopher or architect in question and relates it to their major works.

In the same series

Thomas Mann

Herbert Lehnert and Eva Wessell

REAKTION BOOKS

Published by Reaktion Books Ltd
Unit 32, Waterside
44–48 Wharf Road
London N1 7UX, UK
www.reaktionbooks.co.uk

First published 2019

Printed and bound in Great Britain by Bell & Bain, Glasgow

A catalogue record for this book is available from the British Library

ISBN 978 1 78914 081 1

Contents

Texts and Abbreviations

This book aims to stay close to Thomas Mann's own language. All quotations are taken from the latest German edition of Mann's work together with the equivalent passage of a published translation of our choice, usually the most recent. In case of disagreement, we will substitute our own translation; a 'cf.' following the translation indicates that the text has been altered.

Since some of Mann's works have appeared in English under a range of titles (*Lotte in Weimar*: *The Beloved Returns*; 'Bajazzo': 'The Joker' or 'The Dilettante') or are not translated at all ('Gefallen'), or only partially, as is the case with Mann's diaries, we are using original German titles throughout the text, providing an English translation at a title's first occurrence and occasionally later to enhance clarity. Missing italics accompanying a translated title indicate the lack of an English translation. The same rules govern works by Thomas Mann's brother Heinrich, who is an essential part of the discussion of Mann's early life. The titles of works by other authors are given in English.

References to Thomas Mann's works are incorporated in the text. Those from the new Frankfurt edition (*Große kommentierte Frankfurter Ausgabe der Werke von Thomas Mann*) will appear as FA, followed by Roman numerals indicating the volume number and Arabic numerals indicating the page number. Most numbered volumes, with the exception of two (XXI, XXII), consist of a text and a commentary volume: the text for *Buddenbrooks*, for example, would carry the designation I.I, the commentary volume I.II. Mann's diaries are cited in the text by date. Since the diaries, currently published by the Fischer Publishing House in ten volumes, are slated to be republished as part of *Große kommentierte Frankfurter Ausgabe der Werke von Thomas Mann*, all further information will soon be obsolete.

References to other editions (since the *Frankfurter Ausgabe* is still in progress) and all translations will be preceded by a two-letter code. The first letter refers to the title of the work, the second to the translator's or editor's last name 'BW' would be code for: *Buddenbrooks*, trans. John E. Woods. The Select Bibliography contains the full reference for each text listed below.

BM I–III: *Briefe*, ed. Erika Mann (1961–5)

BW: *Buddenbrooks*, trans. John E. Woods (1993)

CL: *Confessions of Felix Krull, Confidence Man: Memoirs, Part I*, trans. Denver Lindley (1977)

DN: *Death in Venice and other Tales*, trans. Joachim Neugroschel (1998)

DW: *Doktor Faustus*, trans. John E. Woods (1997)

EK I–VI: *Essays*, ed. Hermann Kurzke and Stephan Stachorski (1993–7)

EL: *Essays of Three Decades*, trans. Helen Lowe-Porter (1947)

FA: *Große kommentierte Frankfurter Ausgabe der Werke von Thomas Mann*, ed. Heinrich Detering et al. (2002–)

GW I–XIII: *Gesammelte Werke*, in *Driezehn Bänden*, ed. Hans Bürgin (1960, 1974)

HL: *The Holy Sinner*, trans. Helen Lowe-Porter (1951)

JW: *Joseph and his Brothers*, trans. John E. Woods (2005)

LC: *Thomas Mann's Addresses Delivered at the Library of Congress 1942–1949* (1963)

LL: *Lotte in Weimar: The Beloved Returns*, trans. Helen Lowe-Porter (1990)

LR: *Letters of Heinrich and Thomas Mann, 1900–1949,*
ed. Hans Wysling, trans. Don Renau (1998)

LW: *Letters of Thomas Mann,* trans. and ed. Richard and Clara
Winston (1971)

MW: *The Magic Mountain,* trans. John E. Woods (1995)

NB I, II: *Notizbücher,* ed. Hans Wysling and Yvonne Schmidlin
(1991, 1992)

PL: *Postmasters and Other Papers: Thomas Mann,* trans. Helen
Lowe-Porter (1968)

RC: *Royal Highness,* trans. A. Cecil Curtis (1992)

RM: *Reflections of a Nonpolitical Man,* trans. Walter D. Morris
(1983)

SL I, II: *Stories of a Lifetime,* trans. Helen Lowe-Porter and Willard
R. Trask (1970) (Trask translated only 'The Black Swan'
in vol. II)

Thomas Mann in 1937; photograph by Carl Van Vechton.

Introduction

Thomas Mann was born in 1875 in the northern German Hanseatic town of Lübeck; he died in 1955 in Zurich, Switzerland. He lived through two world wars, was exiled from Germany when the National Socialists seized power in 1933, moved briefly to Switzerland and then moved to the United States in 1938, becoming an American citizen in 1944. His return to Switzerland in 1952 amounted to a second emigration.

The audience for sophisticated literature in the nineteenth century was the class of citizens called *Bildungsbürger*: lawyers, physicians, parsons, many of them civil servants, who were educated in the Gymnasium, the German equivalent of the British grammar school, and in universities. Loyalty to the state contended with a sense of superiority and the traditional freedom conceded to the city dweller, the 'Bürger', a conflict that led to the revolution in most German states in 1848. Following its suppression, the princes of not yet united Germany, aware of the political significance of the *Bildungsbürger* and their importance for the function of government, had allowed broad freedom of literature.

Heinrich and Thomas Mann wrote for the members of this class, addressing their world in their language, even though neither of them had finished Gymnasium. The curriculum appeared old-fashioned and stale to them; they were determined to become modern writers. Both complemented their education by intense self-study. From brother Heinrich, Thomas learned about

Schopenhauer's all-encompassing 'Will' and about Nietzsche's morality of 'Life'. Heinrich owned Schopenhauer's and Nietzsche's works, providing easy access to both philosophers for young Thomas, and Schopenhauer left a deeper impression on him than on his brother. We must take a look at Schopenhauer's and Nietzsche's philosophies.

Schopenhauer started with Immanuel Kant's 'transcendental idealism' (transcendental not meaning approaching the unknown, but as describing the conditions of knowing): space and time are the forms of sensual perception, causality a category of ordering knowledge. Since space, time and causalities happen only in the consciousness of the observer, Kant concluded that we cannot know the reality or essence of things outside of our own consciousness. The 'thing in itself' ('*Ding an sich*') causes us to apply time, space and ordering categories to it.

But can unknown entities construct the world for us? Schopenhauer agreed with Kant that we produce the world as our 'representation' (*Vorstellung*). But it is not a benign one. The objects we meet in our world, which include our bodies, all have the will to exist, making it a place of constant strife and competition. The world of 'representation' we produce, and the world of 'Will' we encounter as part of this world, cannot be separated, nor can a world of continuous combat be understood as obeying a rational order. Schopenhauer understood time and space as being infinite and universal.

Nietzsche's censure of Schopenhauer's pessimistic appraisal of the world and his humanism emphasizing human creativity became a counterweight to Thomas Mann's leaning towards pessimism. Nietzsche proclaimed the 'Will to Power' as a positive life force, dismissing the authority of Christian moral teachings as slave morality. The gods were mere human inventions, and the modern world must be revalued.

While Mann's notebooks date his first reading of Nietzsche to 1894 (*NB* I, 37), traces of contact with Nietzschean philosophy appear in an essay on Heine in his student journal of 1893, about which we will hear more in Chapter One. Mann read Nietzsche critically. A lasting impact was the philosopher's insight that all knowledge is dependent on perspective: there can be no absolute metaphysical certainty. The world of language, Nietzsche had found as early as 1873, consisted merely of a set of symbols and metaphors resting on conventions. For a long time, Thomas Mann's early work was understood as unequivocally conservative. In truth, it has always been open to both the future, in the sense of Nietzschean humanism, and the static view of Schopenhauer's world of representation. He never lost his bias for a paternalistic family order, but it was balanced by his intelligent and determined wife, Katia. Deterministic and progressive tendencies counter one another in his novel *Königliche Hoheit* (1909), where Mann cast benevolent mockery on a minor principality.

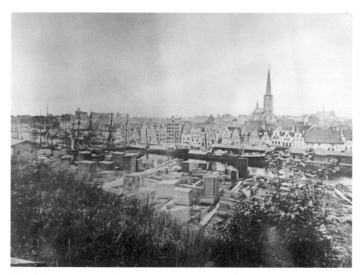

Lübeck, harbour view, *c.* 1870.

Following the victory of liberal, capitalist democracy in the First World War, Mann embraced moderate socialism in the hope that it would eventually humanize the social order. He transferred his hope to Franklin Roosevelt's New Deal after the Manns moved to the United States in 1938; it collapsed after Roosevelt's death, once the United States ended the controlled war economy, returned to the principle of free enterprise and began to engage in the Cold War with the Soviet Union. The Manns left the United States in 1952.

Mann's late essay 'Versuch über Tschechow' (1954; 'Chekhov') concentrates on Chekhov's self-doubt, revealing similar feelings in himself. The essay moves near several religious confessions we have of Mann: 'Fragment über das Religiöse' (Fragment on Religiosity) of 1931, the beginning of 'Meine Zeit' (My Time) of 1950, and 'Lob der Vergänglichkeit' (This I Believe) of 1952. Each time he avoids naming a personal God. In the humorous novel *Joseph und seine Brüder* (1943; Joseph and his Brothers), Abraham's search for the highest deity produces a God of the Whole embracing both good and evil: the traditional personal God is preserved and, at the same time, shown to be a human construct.

During the lifetime of the brothers Mann, the modern world view expanded. Physical science departed from the classical idea of seeing atoms as the basic building blocks of all matter. The duality of light, observable as particles and as waves, was extended to all matter: subatomic particles can be observed as waves; the tangible world consists of intangibles. The modern view of language we find in Thomas Mann's experimental work corresponds to this understanding. Truth depends on context: while never absolute, it is never fully elusive either. Modern literature explores living in the modern world.

1

Thomas Mann, the Outsider Writer, in the Shadow of his Brother

In April 1893, when Thomas Mann was seventeen and still in the tenth grade at the Gymnasium in Lübeck, he learned that he would not be promoted to the next level. It was not a new scenario for him. School bored him, and he neglected his homework; there were always more fascinating things to learn. His model was brother Heinrich, four years his senior and already well on the way to becoming a writer. Heinrich had recently turned to reading philosophy, and the younger brother was following his example. Thomas Mann would gladly have left behind the hated school altogether, but he had to be advanced in order to qualify for the privilege of a one-year voluntary military service. So, he had to shoulder another year of school.

But for now, he was on holiday and could focus on the student magazine he had started with friends. He called it *Der Frühlings-sturm!* (A Blast of Spring!). In the introduction he wrote: 'Yes, as the blast of spring pours into dust-encrusted nature, so will our words and thoughts smash into the dust-encrusted minds and the bloated philistine ignorance that is against us' (*FA* XIV.I, 18).

The first issue of *Der Frühlingssturm!* is lost, but a fellow student, who had preserved his copy, quoted two sentences from a review of Henrik Ibsen's drama *The Master Builder* in a commemorative article. The young Thomas Mann had found the expression 'robust conscience' in the play and applied it to his neglect of doing homework (*FA* XIV.I, 19). The theme of a 'robust conscience' goes

Thomas Mann with his siblings Heinrich, Carla and Julia in Lübeck, *c.* 1885.

to the core of Ibsen's late play where he questioned the modernity his earlier plays had introduced. One of them, the provocative *A Doll's House*, had been performed at the Lübeck theatre two years earlier. Thomas attended the theatre frequently, with and without permission; he would not have missed the play that questioned the traditional family and encouraged him to turn against the 'dust-encrusted minds and the bloated philistine ignorance'.

From the middle of May to 3 July 1893, brother Heinrich stayed with the family in Lübeck. He later confessed to his friend Ludwig Ewers that, instead of working on his novel, he had dallied away the time with Thomas.[1] The brothers had established a close

Julia Mann-da Silva, left, Thomas Mann's mother, 1890s.

relationship, agreeing on their liking for the poet Heinrich Heine. The work of Friedrich Nietzsche protesting against and contradicting the established world view had been of vivid interest to Heinrich since January 1891.[2] Evidence that Thomas shared these new ideas with his brother is provided in his essay 'Heinrich Heine, der "Gute"' (Heinrich Heine, the 'Good' Person) in the second issue of *Der Frühlingssturm!* In it he argues against the moral standard a Lutheran minister had applied to their favourite poet in a Berlin newspaper. Heine, the minister submitted, was a good Christian. But for the young Thomas Mann, Heine was neither 'good' nor a 'Christian', but 'great'. In his opinion, informed by Nietzsche, concepts like 'good' and 'bad' had only social meaning; they were as relative as concepts like 'above' and 'below'. The rebellious student argued that what was considered moral goodness in bourgeois society was a mere mixture of egotism and Christian morality (*FA* XIV.I, 21–3). Heinrich had also studied Schopenhauer and must have shared his interest with his brother.

The relationship between the brothers had not always been harmonious. In Heinrich's correspondence with his friend Ewers – letters that tell us much about Heinrich's readings and literary self-education – we find condescending remarks about fourteen-year-old Thomas's attempts at writing poetry. The younger brother had naively written love poems for a fellow student. Heinrich, asked to critique them, was disturbed by the homoerotic content and declared them worthless. Half a year later, in November 1890, Heinrich again found no value in his brother's lyrical efforts, asking Ewers to convey a single word to him: 'Blödsinn' (foolishness).[3] Thomas must have been severely hurt. Now, in 1893, he impressed Heinrich with his journal *Der Frühlingssturm!* But Thomas most likely never forgot the slights.

Had he lived, Thomas and Heinrich Mann's father would not have approved of his son's student newspaper: he wanted both of his sons to concentrate on their studies. Even though he himself

The 'Haus Beckergrube', home of the Mann family after 1883.

had only scant formal training, he had acquired considerable literary sophistication as an autodidact. He had been selected by his peers to be a member of the senate, the city state's governing body, and called for his oldest son to study law. For his second son he decided on trade; Thomas would become his successor as head of the firm. The senator was not only disappointed by his two older sons' lack of interest in his design for the future of the family firm, but he even doubted that Heinrich had sufficient talent to become a successful writer. In his mind, thorough and formal studies were necessary. The educational record of his second son raised even more doubts.

When Senator Mann died in 1891, Thomas was sixteen and Heinrich twenty. In his will, the father had ordered the dissolution of the firm, requesting the resulting capital to be controlled by executors, not by his widow. Fear of his wife's leniency towards the children seems to have been the motive. He specifically asked that the executors impede Heinrich's plans to become a writer; they applied that admonition to Thomas as well.

Thomas followed Heinrich's aspirations to become a modern writer. In the early 1890s Heinrich had read works by the Viennese novelist and critic Hermann Bahr, who had brought a new writing style from Paris to the German-speaking literati. The movement's leader was the French novelist Paul Bourget. Heinrich applied Bourget's post-naturalist, impressionistic, psychological style to his first novel, *In einer Familie* (1894; In a Family).

In Bourget's novels much attention rests on dilettantes, heirs to their fathers' fortunes, who spent their days probing the enticements of the modern urban world without devoting themselves to anything in particular. Bourget's growing conservatism argued against this inappropriate form of modernity. The brothers Mann were far less well-endowed than the dilettantes in Bourget's novels, but they had also avoided a useful profession and had turned away from the give-and-take of society. They accepted dilettantism as their condition. Heinrich's novel, in progress in 1893, had a wealthy dilettante as a protagonist. An early notebook by Thomas contains evidence that he studied the works of Bourget, Bahr, dilettantism and the new writing style (*NB* 1, 17, 51). *Der Frühlingssturm!* included a prose-poem, 'Vision', that had borrowed the setting from a poem by Heinrich but had transformed it into impressionistic prose. Thomas dedicated it to Hermann Bahr.

In the spring of 1894 Thomas Mann moved to Munich, where Frau Senator Mann had rented an apartment. Interest payments from the remaining assets of their father's firm allowed for a small stipend for both brothers, enabling them to live and travel modestly. The father's will had stipulated a practical vocation. Thomas was apprenticed in an insurance firm, but the work bored him, and he soon abandoned it. An attempt at studying journalism by attending lectures at Munich's Technical University did not last long; he simply wanted to write.

To become a modern writer necessitated a thorough immersion in European literature. Heinrich owned Georg Brandes's *Main Currents in Nineteenth Century Literature: Lectures at the Copenhagen University*, which discussed French, German and English writers. Thomas read all six volumes. Later, in 1900, he bought his own set, which he continued to use. For a time, and to a degree, he shared Heinrich's interest in Bourget and in French literature and history. Thomas seems to have been reluctant to reveal the strength of his brother's early influence; some of his comments about his early studies under-report French influence. But we can be sure that he gained much by reading the works of Émile Zola and the brothers Goncourt and Gustave Flaubert.

Heinrich did not care much for Nordic literature, even though it had become popular in Germany during the 1890s. Thomas, by contrast, read a host of Scandinavian authors in translation: Ibsen's dramas, Norwegian novels of merchant families, *Niels Lyhne* by Jens Peter Jacobsen, outsider novels by Knut Hamsun. With this

Thomas (right) and Heinrich Mann in Munich, *c*. 1900.

preference he took a step back from his brother's involvement with French and Italian culture.

Although he knew and agreed that modern literature had to be post-Romantic, he also chose to include Novalis, Franz Brentano, Friedrich Schlegel and E.T.A. Hoffmann in his reading list. The German Romantics always remained of interest to him and influenced his writing. And there was Goethe: an early notebook entry of 1894 expresses his admiration. Mann studied Johann Peter Eckermann's *Conversations with Goethe* then and several times throughout his life.

A lasting educational experience was his love for Richard Wagner's music that began in Lübeck during his school days. Hanno Buddenbrook's rapturous response to *Lohengrin* is certainly autobiographical. His Wagner enthusiasm was checked to a degree by Nietzsche's criticism in *The Case of Wagner*; the treatise both amused him and made him assume a critical distance to Wagner.

Thomas Mann wrote his first story, 'Gefallen' (1894; Fallen), during his first year in Munich. The plot centres on the protagonist's affair with an actress based on the young Ida Hofmann, whom Mann had repeatedly seen performing at Munich's Royal Theatre. He wrote a letter to her, which is preserved, asking for a visit. She did not respond; the young Thomas wrote the story of a successful affair instead.

But that was not the only incentive for writing 'Gefallen'; another came from an unpublished story by Heinrich named 'Haltlos' (Unsteady), which presented an example of how morality in bourgeois society depends on a person's material means. At one point, during a visit to a house of prostitution, the protagonist wonders if he should consider himself 'fallen' in the manner of a 'fallen' woman.

'Gefallen' is largely forgotten or, at least, undervalued. Thomas Mann himself did not include it in any of his story collections. But it shows the nineteen-year-old as an observer of the moral changes of his time, changes that are still continuing in the twenty-first century. He started out as a modernist writer, not in the sense of an avant-gardist who is aiming for an unusual style, but rather in the sense of a writer focused on changes in his social environment.

During a bohemian dinner party, an idealistic, progressive student asks, as did Heinrich's protagonist in 'Haltlos', if a promiscuous man also deserves to be called 'fallen'. A Doctor Selten, while still a student, had composed a letter to a young actress, lauding her performance, winning her over. Free love for the doctor ends, however, when the woman becomes a highly paid prostitute, claiming that she needs the money, and that bourgeois virtues do not match her profession. The doctor, admitting that he told his own story, concludes: 'A woman who falls for love today, will fall for money tomorrow' (*FA* II.I, 49). While his words sound cynical, misogynistic and final, the text counters this judgement. Fragrance from lilacs in a vase stirs the memory of the protagonist because lilacs bloomed on the way to his beloved: he still values his love. The young writer ends his story on an ambivalent note. Ambivalence was to become a hallmark of Thomas Mann's literary production.

'Gefallen' belongs to a literary movement that demanded candid representation of sexual issues and feelings. George Bernard Shaw's play *Mrs Warren's Profession* was written in 1893; its performance was banned until 1902. In the United States, Stephen Crane's *Maggie: A Girl of the Streets* appeared in print in 1893. 'Gefallen' was published in 1894 in *Die Gesellschaft*, a journal for new literature, in the same year it was written.

A good source for information on the years in which Thomas Mann's writing skills developed – from 1894 to the publication of *Buddenbrooks* in 1901 – are his letters to Otto Grautoff, who had finished school the same year as Thomas and was apprenticed to a bookseller in the small town of Brandenburg. Mann's letters to Grautoff allow insight into the way he handled his homoerotic inclinations. Unfortunately, the correspondence is incomplete: Grautoff's answers are lost and some letters are edited, probably because of embarrassing content. Grautoff loved his friend.

Thomas had been attracted to fellow students. His first homo-erotic experience was a passion for a schoolmate when both were about fourteen. He showed a poem to the friend, expressing his love. It was coldly dismissed (*BM* III, 387). The second time he fell in love with an acquaintance from school he had learned to be more cautious. He merely borrowed a pencil, an episode that grew into a motif in *Der Zauberberg* (1924; *The Magic Mountain*, *FA* v.i, 183–9; *MW*, 117–19).

Only with Grautoff could Mann share the feelings of his passion, but he could also behave condescendingly towards him. When Grautoff, also aspiring to a literary career, shared his attempts, Thomas declared them somewhat promising but not yet adequate. There seems to have been a need for this kind of disparagement: it allowed him to feel superior to Grautoff. He might also shed his role of inferiority towards Heinrich. He might also have wanted to prove to Grautoff, and to himself, that he could control his homoerotic inclinations.

Grautoff confided in his friend, telling him that he was unhappy with the book trade and had thought of an acting career. Mann suggested, being satirical, that Grautoff play Juliet in Shakespeare's *Romeo and Juliet*, implying that he might be a natural at portraying the lead's sexual desire in her monologue. Grautoff must have expressed his enamoured feelings to Mann at home in Lübeck.

Sometimes Mann could assure Grautoff of his most intimate friendship, calling him the only person with whom he could communicate without shame (*FA* xxi, 42, 49–50). But he was worried when his friend considered hypnotic treatment. Grautoff had consulted an assistant of the psychologist Dr Albert Moll, whose book on homosexuality Thomas had read.[4] He was concerned about Grautoff's encounters with the members of the Berlin school of psychiatry, who often published case studies: Grautoff's case might become included in such a study and expose him. But he did not consider treatment for himself. In early summer of 1895, he corresponded with Grautoff about a visit to Berlin. Despite his friend's enthusiasm, Mann suddenly changed plans and travelled to Rome to spend time with Heinrich. He may have feared Grautoff's affection.

Heinrich had been hired as an editor for the monthly *Das Zwanzigste Jahrhundert* (The Twentieth Century). While the paper was published in Berlin, he was allowed to do his editorial work wherever he chose. The journal was politically conservative, nationalistic and anti-Semitic, but it aspired to cover more general cultural ground. Heinrich appears to have accepted the prevailing bias of the journal in the hope of emphasizing its cultural interest element and to gain experience in journalism. But soon the journal contained abrasive anti-Semitic editorials by him. These editorials overstepped the degree of prejudice common in the social class to which both brothers belonged and might have been written under pressure from owners or investors. Thomas helped his brother with the journal; he wrote a few reviews that, to a degree, followed the bias of the paper. In private, both brothers treated Jewish citizens as Others, but they were neither partisan nor actively anti-Semitic; both would marry women from Jewish backgrounds.

Before Thomas joined his brother in Rome, he visited Venice and a few other places in central Italy. Several texts he composed during his first Italian visit in 1894 and 1895 are not preserved. We know of titles of a few short stories from letters to Grautoff. Thomas might have discarded them because they did not pass muster with Heinrich. One of these lost stories, 'Begegnung' (Encounter), might have been rewritten after his stay in Venice in late 1896 or early 1897 as 'Enttäuschung' (Disillusionment; *FA* II.I, 79–86; *SL* I, 29–34).

The narrator enjoys a morning of 'incomparably bright and festive beauty' at St Mark's Square in Venice, as Nietzsche evoked it in his poem 'My Happiness' (or 'My Bliss') from the 'Songs of the Prince Vogelfrei' in *The Gay Science*. The narrator's gay moment is countered by a German-speaking stranger complaining of his disappointment with life. Having grown up in a parsonage absorbing the dichotomous rhetoric of the pulpit, he expected rigid dualities like good and evil to explain the world. This basic orientation was lost, replaced by grandiose expectations found in the words of the poets. But reality set in, leading to disappointment. The view of the ocean is limited by a horizon, but even within the horizon disillusionment abounds; the actual nature of things cannot be seen: 'What is it, actually?' is his repeated question, for which he finds no answer. The piece reflects the absence of a basic orientation in modernity, the need to live with contradictions and much that is unknowable. The stranger suffers from Schopenhauer's pessimism; the narrator enjoys Nietzsche's Venetian happiness. The text became part of Thomas Mann's first collection of novellas, *Der kleine Herr Friedemann* (1898).

Thomas's second published story was 'Der Wille zum Glück' (1896; The Will for Happiness). The story does not allude to Nietzsche's 'Will to Power'; rather it questions the artist's desire for an ordinary bourgeois life that, for him, is forbidden. An artist must be a superior outsider; he must not seek ordinary happiness. The story is conveyed by a first-person narrator observing Paolo Hofmann, a school friend and outsider like himself, whose outsider status is marked by a heart ailment, and who is kept alive by devotion to his art of painting. But his talent vanishes once he falls in love with an attractive Jewish woman. The narrator observes Paolo's erotic energy when he visits the beloved with Paolo. Paolo's face, though seemingly tranquil, appears to resemble a lurking animal, ready to strike (*FA* II.I, 55, 57; *DN*, 7, 9). Schopenhauer's 'Will' is at work. While Paolo, waiting for permission to marry, manages to focus his will on his survival, once married he dies, practically on the wedding night. An underlying premise of this story is that erotic desire, an outgrowth of the 'Will', can be transformed into art.

The theme of transforming sexual energy into art seems to be similar to Freud's concept of sublimation, but it is not derived from it, nor does it involve the subconscious. Both Freud and

Mann were influenced by Schopenhauer. Mann did not read Freud's works until 1925.

'Der Wille zum Glück' was published in 1896 in *Simplicissimus*, a journal founded as a literary weekly by the Langen Publishing House where Thomas worked as an editor.

In spite of the sudden success with 'Gefallen', it took Mann several years before his reputation as a writer was established. He had failed to place two completed manuscripts with a magazine. The first, a story named 'Walter Weiler', a fictional diary by a young man who transforms himself into an outsider, he would rewrite in 1897 as 'Der Bajazzo'.[5] It is about a young man who decides to live alone, supported by his inheritance, but when he is attracted to a woman his arrogant detachment from life becomes a misfortune. The other manuscript, 'Der kleine Professor', composed right after 'Gefallen', was probably rewritten as 'Der kleine Herr Friedemann' (1897; Little Herr Friedemann).

Johannes Friedemann is forced into an existence as an outsider by a deformity, a hunchback, triggered by an intoxicated nurse who let him fall off a nursing table. Thomas Mann had found the motif of a child crippled by such a fall in Henrik Ibsen's *Little Eyolf*, a drama where female sexual desire is shown in conflict with responsibility. Mann had taken another motif from Theodor Fontane's novel *Effi Briest*, which he had read in 1985, the year of its publication (*FA* xxi, 73). The pharmacist Gieshübler does not dare to love because he is misshapen, nearly a hunchback, and he takes, similar to Friedemann, the enjoyment of art as a compensation for missing love. While Fontane lets Gieshübler lead a satisfied existence, Mann has his protagonist demonstrate how little the devotion to art can make up for the loss of love.[6]

Friedemann falls in love with Gerda, an emancipated outsider despised by the town's women. During a performance of Richard Wagner's opera *Lohengrin*, Gerda plays with Friedemann's infatuation and continues to do so at a party in her house. When she inquires about his condition, Friedemann abandons his restraint, confessing his love. But she does not want a relationship with a cripple and pushes him down. Rejected and lying on the ground, he crawls to the river, moving his upper body into the shallow water. He drowns, overcoming his will to live. Thomas Mann lets Friedemann enter into the timeless and spaceless realm of Schopenhauer's 'Will', into the *Weltgrund*, the 'base of the world', as he once called Schopenhauer's principle (*EK* IV, 254).[7] But Schopenhauer's belief that devoting oneself to art negates the 'Will', and thus offers refuge from suffering, fails to help little Herr Friedemann.

A passage in Mann's novel *Joseph in Ägypten* (1936; *Joseph in Egypt*) connects Mut-em-enet's (Potiphar's wife's) passion for Joseph with 'Der Tod in Venedig' (1912; Death in Venice) and 'Der kleine Herr Friedemann'. The narrator (in this case speaking for the author) explains that these three passages expressed the motif of visitation (*Heimsuchung*): love breaks into a well-ordered life with destructive force. Visitation is a basic motif of Thomas Mann's writing, revealing a lifelong vulnerability. Johannes Friedemann, and possibly Gerda, suffer from repressed erotic feelings. In two letters to Otto Grautoff, Mann mentioned his satisfaction with 'Der kleine Herr Friedemann'. The story had allowed him to express himself through forms and masks, and shackles had fallen off (*FA* XXI, 89, 95–6). In February 1896 Thomas let Grautoff know that he had burned his secret diaries and recommended that his friend do the same (*FA* XXI, 73). Now he could talk in fictional stories about his problems without exposing himself.

'Der kleine Herr Friedemann' was completed in September 1896 (*FA* XXI, 78). The author sent his text to *Neue deutsche Rundschau*, a step upward. This journal, with high cultural ambitions, was owned by the publishing firm Samuel Fischer in Berlin, which published the story in 1897; Samuel Fischer himself became interested in the new author.

In October 1896 Thomas went to Italy again. After spending two weeks in Venice, he settled in Rome in late November, renting his own apartment. But the brothers kept in contact, and Heinrich most likely resumed his old role as tutor. When Thomas arrived in Rome, Heinrich was writing 'Eine wohltätige Frau' (A Charitable Woman; not published during his lifetime). In it an emancipated woman marries an impotent man with the intention of defrauding concupiscent men. Much of Thomas Mann's novella 'Luischen' (Little Lizzy), written in the summer of 1897, takes up Heinrich's theme of an unlikely couple. Much later, Thomas mentioned that 'Luischen' was one of the first of his stories that had impressed Heinrich, an indication that the brother must have criticized Thomas's earlier work (*FA* XXI, 386f.; *LR*, 90).

The narrator of 'Luischen' assumes a marked distance to the narrated events. Amra, the protagonist, needs her marriage to an impotent husband to cover up her affairs. Her name is that of a hetaera, a high-class prostitute in the story of Buddha, for whose life Thomas had recently developed an interest. Amra humiliates Jacoby, her loving but impotent and oddly deformed husband, by forcing him to publicly perform a dance in the role of a lascivious young woman. The victim's shortcomings are grotesquely inverted, amusing an audience of friends. Amra's lover, composing the music for Jacoby's dance, fits some bars reminiscent of Richard Wagner's musical drama *Tristan und Isolde* into his otherwise banal composition. Hearing the music from the drama of love, Jacoby suddenly grasps the reality of his being betrayed and dies on the spot.

Mann had difficulties placing this novella with a publisher; *Neue deutsche Rundschau* did not want it. It was finally published in 1900 in *Die Gesellschaft*, the same journal that had printed 'Gefallen'. In 1903 it became part of the story collection *Tristan*.

'Tobias Mindernickel', also written in the summer of 1897, is a self-mocking projection of the author in old age after a failed writing career. Mann gave his own initials to his character and belittles him by an aptronym; 'minder' means minor and 'nickel' is a low value coin. Mindernickel buys a dog for company and names him Esau, after the twin brother of Jacob in Genesis who, being a few minutes older, claims the right as the first born, and then sells his first-born rights to Jacob. Mindernickel loves the dog but demands strict obedience, eventually killing him when the dog fails to comply. Mindernickel regrets his deed and, like St Peter in Matthew 26:75, weeps 'bitterly'. In German 'weinte bitterlich' (*FA* ii.i, 192; cf. *DN*, 62) recalls a recitative in Johann Sebastian Bach's 'St Matthew Passion': Peter weeps because he has betrayed the Master. The naming of the dog Esau and his killing may allude to the relationship between the brothers that, by 1897, had begun to show strains. 'Tobias Mindernickel' was published in 1898 in *Neue deutsche Rundschau* and in the same year in the collection *Der kleine Herr Friedemann*.

2

From *Buddenbrooks*, a Novel of Liberation, to *Fiorenza*, a Play of Power

In June 1897 a letter from Samuel Fischer, his publisher, encouraged Thomas Mann to write a novel. During that summer, while still writing stories, he registered ideas and family memories in his notebook, intended for a novel about the decline of a family. He had just witnessed such a decline: the dissolution of the family firm with painful losses. Were both brothers, living in Rome and busily writing, guilty of its fate? Should they have remained in Lübeck, learned the wholesale trade and continued on with the firm? But both brothers no longer identified with the businessmen of Lübeck, the grand burghers. As writers, they wished to join and address the class of educated citizens, the *Bildungsbürger*. Thomas found a way to distance himself from feelings of guilt: invent a family-owned business held for generations and have it fail because the principals, over time, had become weary with their lives in business. Decline, decadence and degeneration were fashionable subjects among young writers of the time, who were questioning the power of their fathers and their bourgeois traditions.

Buddenbrooks begins with eight-year-old Antonie Buddenbrook, called Tony throughout the book, having her knowledge of Martin Luther's Small Catechism examined. The very first words in the novel are: 'Was ist das' ('What does this mean' without a question mark: *FA* I.I, 9; *BW*, 5). Tony has just recited the first article of faith: the belief in God, the creator. Now she stumbles over the question of its meaning. Her grandfather has made young Tony recite the catechism with the intention of mocking the claim that God had created house, land and foodstuff. Playfully offering to do business with her, he makes the point that in the modern world these things are bought and sold as commodities; they are no longer venerated as God's creations.

The novel ends with Tony doubting the Christian promise of an eternal life, popularly understood as a reunion, a *Wiedersehen*, in the hereafter. Only the aged teacher Sesemi Weichbrodt affirms this hope. She has wrested her conviction from the many doubts the rational teacher in her has raised. 'So it is,' she proclaims, standing upright (*FA* I.I, 837; *BW*, 648). Is this the answer to the initial question: 'What does this mean'? Or should the reader regard her fight against reason with irony? The question is left open.

Johann Buddenbrook, the head of the family and its business, is seventy. He has greatly increased the value of the firm, evident by the patrician house whose purchase the family celebrates in the first part of the novel. He conducts himself as a harmless and jovial person; his well-meaning face is seemingly incapable of expressing malice (*FA* I.I, 10; *BW*, 6). But at dinner's end, he turns out to be a different person. He has excluded Gotthold, the son of his first marriage, from the family, because Gotthold has married a shop-keeper's daughter against his wishes. The elder Buddenbrook was driven by the ambition that his family should rise to the first circle of the city republic's families.

To add to his rank as burgher, Johann Buddenbrook had bought a house in the best location in town. It is destined to contain the offices of the firm and will become part of the inheritance for his business partner and successor: the second son, also named Johann or Jean. In response, Gotthold sends a letter claiming compensation for a reduced inheritance. Yet the elder Buddenbrook refuses. Paying the compensation would restore peace in the family, but the firm would lose capital and love must not get in the way of money.

The Mann family residence in Mengstrasse, Lübeck, before 1883 – the location of most of the *Buddenbrooks* fiction.

He himself had married his second wife for her dowry and had insisted that his second son marry the daughter of the wealthiest family in the town.

This second son has grown into a Christian believer in contrast to his father, who identifies with the Enlightenment. The scene in which the elder Buddenbrook discusses Gotthold's claim with Jean shows how much the potential loss of capital outweighs the concern for peace in the family; Gotthold, in need of money for his three marriageable daughters' dowries, will remain an outcast. The determination of the older Buddenbrook, and the complicity of the younger one in the exclusive focus on the well-being of the firm, establish the standard for what we will call the 'hard burgher': a businessman whose decisions are motivated by the prospect of profit without regard for human suffering. The necessity to act as a 'hard burgher' will be one important theme in *Buddenbrooks*.

After Jean inherits the wholesale business, he conducts it in the belief that the firm is under God's protection. When a businessman courts his daughter, Jean easily approves; the suitor is a pastor's son who had presented himself as a pious Christian. When Tony resists, her father goes as far as to engage the pastor of their church to admonish young women who defy their parents. The suitor, merely out for the dowry, becomes insolvent in a few years. His father-in-law could save him, but the necessary funds would have torn into the Buddenbrook firm's capital. In one of the most striking scenes in the novel, Jean shows himself relieved when he discovers that his daughter has never loved her husband. It makes it easier to abandon his son-in-law, even if it means dissolving a Christian marriage (*FA* 1.1, 237–9; *BW*, 191–3). Jean has fulfilled the role of a 'hard burgher'.

Jean's business sense has overcome his Christian sentiments. Perhaps worse, it has caused him to disregard the feelings of his daughter. The scenes showing her with Morten Schwarzkopf while on holiday in Travemünde on the Baltic coast belong to the most moving parts of the novel. In one such incident, the lovers gaze at the sea, unobstructed all the way to the horizon. They perceive the vista in front of them as a symbol of freedom from bourgeois restrictions (*FA* 1.1, 153; cf. *BW*, 124). But the student of medicine has only a middle-class background, and Tony's father is not prepared to take her feelings seriously. Under his pressure, she sacrifices herself for the success and glory of the Buddenbrook firm and family.

Tony keeps her frustrated love for Morten alive, remembering his words and reciting them throughout the narrative. Obvious in her youth, her intelligence would have had a chance to develop through contact with her educated lover and husband; her marriage to an uncaring man dooms her to a life of idleness. Her limitations are sometimes comical, but they contribute to an accusation: her forced marriage has curtailed her development.

Tony's brother Thomas, the heir to the firm, will become senator of the town, a member of the city government, elevating the reputation of the family. He himself has also sacrificed on the altar of family reputation. He loved Anna, a sales girl from a flower shop, and she shared his affection. Both understand that Anna's social class prevents her from becoming his wife. A scene, depicting Anna's visit at Thomas's bier, assures the reader of her lasting affection. The theme of impeded love is central to the bourgeois order and to the novel.

Genuine love can exist outside of that order: Kai Graf Mölln, the son of an impoverished nobleman, sought the friendship and affection of Hanno, the only child of Senator Buddenbrook. How much he is devoted to him becomes apparent when Hanno, on his deathbed and no longer able to recognize his family members, smiles at him (*FA* 1.1, 836; *BW*, 648).

The theme of decline becomes more dominant towards the end of the novel. Hanno's friend Kai, planning to become a writer, observes the Buddenbrook family for signs of decay. Christian

Buddenbrook, Thomas' and Tony's brother, would become his most obvious example. He has a talent for imitation; perhaps he would have succeeded as an actor. But the family tradition requires him to go into business, where he fails. Thomas, the senator, is gifted but discontented.

Before his early death, the senator discovers a semi-religious comfort: Arthur Schopenhauer's essay 'On Death and its Relation to the Indestructibility of Our Inner Nature'. Thomas understands Schopenhauer's explanation of death as merging the self, the soul, into the indestructible all-encompassing 'Will' with the possibility of emerging as another – better – human being. But the comfort does not last. Thomas soon finds this substitute religion an improper one for his position as grand burgher and senator. Soon afterwards he has a stroke and falls into the gutter, where he dies hours later. His death is described as the ugliest of several death scenes in the novel.

Does the novel offer a comfort? Do the male Buddenbrooks, while in decline as merchants, rise in human status? Jean Buddenbrook wants to go beyond his father's rationalism, having become a believing Christian, but his business sense conflicts with Christian charity. His son Thomas, apprenticed in his father's business at sixteen, cannot pursue his literary interests. Hanno, the last of the male Buddenbrooks, plays the piano, but remains a dilettante and lacks the will to live. The mercantile tradition seems to exclude individual growth.

As much as the theme of decline dominates the novel, it is meant not to sadden the reader but rather to elicit sympathy. The narrator often takes the perspective of a family member, inviting readers to participate in the family's life. At the end of Chapter Six of Part Ten, for example, Thomas's weariness is counteracted by Tony's sisterly gesture: as both look at the Baltic Sea, Thomas carries on about the monotony of the waves, rolling drearily and senselessly towards the shore, yet comforting him with their simplicity and necessity. The words reveal the anticipation of his death. Tony feels ashamed for her brother: 'One does not say something like that,' she thinks. But to compensate for having felt ashamed for him, 'she pulls his arm into hers' (*FA* I.I, 741; *BW*, 578).

A contrast to this affection can be found in the deteriorating relationship between the brothers Christian and Thomas, as they clash in the second chapter of Part Nine over the distribution of objects inherited after their mother's death. But Thomas Mann has distributed features of both brothers to the two opponents in his text, carefully avoiding identification.

We know that tensions arose between the brothers after their return to Rome from Palestrina, where, during the summer of 1897, Thomas had made plans for his family novel. In a draft for an unsent letter, written in 1918, Heinrich describes a scene in his apartment in 1897: Thomas, then 22 and sitting in front of the piano (probably playing Wagner chords), casually turns back to Heinrich with the words, 'In inimicos' (against the enemies) (*FA* XXII, 714; cf. *LR*, 127).[1] Thomas probably meant the enemies of Wagner, Heinrich among them.

A reason for the slowly developing discord between the brothers in Rome in 1898 may have been that Thomas had started writing his family novel without involving Heinrich. They had talked in Palestrina about a satire about their home town, using family members as models. There may also have been plans to work together, as Heinrich remembered much later; he may have expected closer cooperation in producing the novel.[2] Heinrich started to write his own novel *Im Schlaraffenland* (1900; In the Land of Cockaigne) instead. It involves Jewish bankers and stockbrokers in Berlin, treating the acquisition of money satirically; he may also have wished to distance himself from his family heritage in business.

Satire was not alien to Thomas. *Buddenbrooks* contains satirical sections: the chapter describing Hanno's day at school, the account of the Lübeck revolution, the deprecatory portrait of clergymen. But *Buddenbrooks* balances satire with a sympathetic representation of family relations, while *Im Schlaraffenland* is harshly one-dimensional in its depiction of a Jewish banker in his pursuit of cultural assimilation by promoting and protecting aspiring non-Jewish authors. The characters' private lives are as appalling as their business practices.

A document revealing Heinrich's criticism of his younger brother is the short story 'Doktor Biebers Versuchung' (1898; Doctor Bieber's Temptation). Heinrich wrote the piece early in 1898 while Thomas was still in Rome, taking aim at two of his brother's predilections, Wagner and Schopenhauer, putting them both down. Patients in a sanatorium idolize Wagner's music; a physician boasts of the power of his mind, misusing the idea of Schopenhauer's metaphysical 'Will'.

Thomas left Rome on 22 April 1898. Heinrich accompanied him to his beloved Florence where both dined together, perhaps a conciliatory gesture by the older brother. But tensions persisted, even though they must have tried to ignore or repair them; letters from that period are not preserved. The first letter, of 24 October 1900, by Thomas to his brother (*FA* XXI, 129–31) is friendly. Evidence of continued strain, however, surfaces in a letter of 5 December 1903 (*FA* XXI, 239–50; *LR*, 53–8), in which Thomas criticizes Heinrich's novel *Die Jagd nach Liebe* (*The Hunt for Love*), accusing him of distorted language and the use of sexual scenes merely for effect. The harsh censure in this letter is surprising for Thomas Mann's usual conciliatory epistolary style. It conveys the impression that a dammed-up resentment, perhaps held since 1898, has been released. Thomas has moved away from Heinrich's dominance.

When the brothers visited Florence in the spring of 1898, four centuries had passed since Girolamo Savonarola's objections to the cult of beauty and the reawakening of paganism. The monk interested Thomas; he had risen to the position of spiritual ruler simply through the power of his words. The opportunity to understand Savonarola's rise in terms of Nietzsche's essay 'What do Ascetic Ideals Mean?' in *On the Genealogy of Morals* probably delivered additional enticement; there Nietzsche links the spiritual renunciation of sexuality by priests to their control over the self and others. Suppressing his sexuality, Savonarola transfers the latent energy into words and gains control over Florence. Transferring sexual energy into words was a very personal matter for Thomas Mann. The Savonarola project embodied a major new undertaking. But first *Buddenbrooks* had to be finished.

After the trip to Florence, Thomas rejoined his mother and siblings in Munich; his friend Otto Grautoff moved there in the following year. A schoolmate, Korfiz Holm, who had become the manager of the publishing house Albert Langen, employed him as junior editor. He soon made friends; in his own life, Mann did not match the type of outsider he had depicted in his early stories.

In November 1898 he interrupted *Buddenbrooks* for six days to write 'Der Kleiderschrank' (1899; The Wardrobe), a fairy tale welded onto a realistic frame and published in *Neue deutsche Rundschau* in 1899. In places it reads like a symbolist text. The narration limits itself to the perspective of one person, the travelling Albrecht van der Qualen ('Qual' means intense pain in German), whose physicians have given him only a few months to live. He reacts to the diagnosis by refusing to be determined by time and place, the foundation of all perception according to the philosopher Immanuel Kant, and the basis of Schopenhauer's philosophy. Travelling in an express train, he awakens in an unknown city and disembarks, glad that he has lost his sense of space as well.

The realistic narration about the traveller walking into town and renting rooms in the suburb is underlaid with allusions to myth and fairy tale: a lone man, rowing a boat from its stern, suggests Charon, the ferryman to the underworld. When the narrator, seemingly needlessly, interjects that van der Qualen does not wear galoshes (*FA* II.1, 196; *SL* I, 84), he suggests that his character experiences a variant of Hans Christian Andersen's tale of the 'Galoshes of Fortune'. Andersen's galoshes carry the wearer to any place or time he wishes, but van der Qualen has lost the sense of time and place. The landlady, from whom he rents two simple rooms, looks like a character by E.T.A. Hoffmann, the author of fantastic tales (*FA* II.I, 198; *SL*.I, 85).

To his surprise, van der Qualen finds a nude girl in the wardrobe of his rented room. She tells him love stories that end not only unhappily, but cruelly. Addicted to her tales, his heart turns calmer. But is he healed? The story does not tell us; rather it suggests, at last leaving van der Qualen's point of view, that he was dreaming as his train carried him across the mountains.

The Langen publishing house, Mann's place of employment, produced the literary satirical weekly *Simplicissimus*. For this journal he wrote 'Gerächt' (1899; A Revenge), a story about an unsightly but stalwart woman who defends her dignity, and 'Der Weg zum Friedhof' (1900; The Road to the Churchyard), another outsider story on the verge of being a satire. The narrator confronts an older and miserable pedestrian with a youthful blonde cyclist whom the text simply calls Life ('das Leben'). Perhaps the cyclist is a portrait of Thomas Mann's new friend, Paul Ehrenberg, with whom he enjoyed touring together. We will hear more of Paul below and in the next chapter.

The Munich opera often staged the works of Richard Wagner; Mann did not miss performances of *Tristan und Isolde* (*FA* XXI, 121). One of his great stories, simply called 'Tristan', originated during the first months of 1901, while Mann was captivated by his homoerotic attraction to Paul Ehrenberg, a feeling that Paul could only counter with friendship. 'Tristan' is one of Thomas Mann's representations of unattainable love, as are 'Der kleine Herr Friedemann', 'Luischen' and Tony Buddenbrook's love for Morten.

An incentive for the action in 'Tristan' was provided by a scene in Gabriele D'Annunzio's novel *The Triumph of Death* (1894), which had appeared in 1899 in German in *Neue deutsche Rundschau*. In the novel, piano music from Richard Wagner's *Tristan und Isolde* leads a lover to commit a murder–suicide. The grandiosity of the novel, whose author was at the height of his fame, may have lured Thomas to write a parody. The protagonist and lover in 'Tristan', Detlev Spinell, is a writer-outsider with only a single novel to his credit. He resembles his author in carefully choosing his words when writing a letter, but his physical appearance is a caricature. That Spinell comes from Lemberg in Galicia, part of the Austro-Hungarian Empire, signals that he is Jewish, for Mann often a way to indicate alienation. 'Tristan' is set in a sanatorium, probably as a parody of the sanatorium in Heinrich's 'Doctor Bieber's Temptation', the story that had made fun of Thomas's predilection for Wagner and Schopenhauer. In both texts, a female character is named Gabriele, perhaps also a play on D'Annunzio's first name.

Spinell's aesthetic sensibility is captured by the beauty of Gabriele, a patient suffering from tuberculosis. She is the wife of the wholesale trader Klöterjahn, who lives by the Baltic Sea, suggesting Lübeck, the town of *Buddenbrooks*. Spinell seduces Gabriele by making her perform parts of Wagner's *Tristan und Isolde* on the piano, although use of the instrument had been prohibited by her physician for health reasons. Music and text conjure up love and death as doorways into Schopenhauer's 'Will' (*FA* II.I, 352; *DN*, 133). Before Gabriele dies, Spinell accuses Klöterjahn of having reduced his sensitive and talented wife to his ordinary and banal existence. But, with his help, he insists in a poetic letter, she has overcome her plight, is now rising from the 'depth of her degradation and, proud and blissful, perishing under the lethal kiss of beauty' (*FA* II.I, 362; cf. *DN*, 141). The husband, Spinell's letter in hand, takes him to task, reducing him to a cowardly figure. But the scene ends with a message that Gabriele is humming the motif of longing from *Tristan und Isolde* while dying. The aesthete seems to be winning, but he is cut down to size on encountering the vivid laughter of Klöterjahn's robust infant.

Thomas Mann and Paul Ehrenberg cycling near Munich, *c.* 1900.

'Tristan' contains ironic and humorous passages that contrast with the reverence that scenes from Wagner's *Tristan und Isolde* receive, when Gabriele performs on the piano or Spinell interprets the opera. Such contrasts are characteristic of Thomas Mann's style. The novella was published in 1903 in a new volume of collected stories with 'Tristan' as its title piece.

In December 1900 Thomas decided to put the Savonarola material into dramatic form (*FA* XXI, 139; *LR*, 42), but he soon realized that the subject required much research. Less preparation was needed for an experiment that would place a Savonarola figure into contemporary Munich. The action of the story, 'Gladius Dei' (1902), is preceded by three pages, reminiscent of a prose poem, eulogizing the 'luminous' capital of Bavaria, rich in art. For a while, the city appears to be the protagonist, but irony soon appears: Munich's inhabitants worship art and beauty; they take aestheticism as their religion. (This was only true for bohemians; the real Munich remained traditional.)

The story starts with Hieronymus – German for Girolamo – walking from Schwabing, Munich's bohemian district, into town, where he encounters the copy of a painting of a Madonna in the display window of an art shop. While the image entices him erotically, divine inspiration urges him to return to the store to protest the 'light-hearted' and 'supercilious' sense of beauty (*FA* II.I, 230–31; cf. *DN*, 92). Unlike his model, the Florentine Savonarola, Hieronymus proves powerless and is evicted from the premises. He can merely wish for the Sword of God, 'Gladius Dei', to come down upon the city.

Typical of Thomas Mann is the inner contradiction in Hieronymus, who bravely disregards his erotic excitement when he tries to persuade the store's owner to remove the image from his display. The figure of Hieronymus could be read as a revenant of the real Savonarola who is unable to develop his power in Munich, or as a modern bohemian acting in the mask of the Italian Renaissance preacher. The art shop represents modernity in the industrial age of reproduction; the Madonna in the display is merely a black and white photograph of a painting. The text plays to the prejudices of readers who took Modernism as industrially produced imitations promoted by Jews. The art dealer has an Ashkenazi name and a 'Jewish' nose (*FA* II.I, 233; cf. *DN*, 94). 'Gladius Dei' was first published in 1902 in the Viennese weekly *Die Zeit*; it was included in the collection *Tristan* of 1903.

Mann began writing the play *Fiorenza* in early 1903. For sources he relied, among others, on Jacob Burckhardt's *The Civilization of the Renaissance in Italy* (1860) and Pasquale Villari's *Life and Times of Girolamo Savonarola* (1859–61). Burckhardt sees in the Renaissance the advent of modern individualism, a time when educated Italians were turning away from the Church, but he respects Savonarola despite judging him a primitive thinker. By contrast, Villari downplays the monk's lack of education, regarding him as a spiritual hero and Catholic reformer. Protestants claim Savonarola as their own, an opinion shared by Thomas Mann. Marginal notes in his copy of the German translation of Villari's book prove his strong disagreement with the Italian Catholic biographer.[3] Mann read the biography for historical detail, keeping in mind Nietzsche's concept of sexual asceticism as a source of power. One detail mentioned by Villari seems to have confirmed Nietzsche's theory for Mann: the young Savonarola was rejected by a noble girl. Thomas was convinced that Savonarola's reach for power was generated by the sexual energy released when the girl rejected him; Villari had mentioned the rejection only in passing.

The Berlin star critic, Alfred Kerr, lambasted the play after its performance in Berlin in 1903 because it was overloaded with historical particulars. Indeed, the play shows that Mann might have had the ambition to paint a broad picture of the Renaissance. But the climactic scene when 'the Prior' Savonarola seizes power from Lorenzo de' Medici on his deathbed is fictional. In the play, the modernist Lorenzo replaces the Christian religion with the worship of art. But the artists who appear on stage are not worthy of such a claim; they are more interested in self-promotion. Lorenzo venerates Plato religiously, but when he feels death approaching, Plato fails him; for injustices committed in his wars, he needs the Christian God's forgiveness. Thus he calls for Savonarola, who uses the opportunity to gain power.

The first act presents the question of whether there is a need for a new moral foundation. The classicist Poliziano, educator of the young Giovanni de' Medici, who will become Pope Leo X, prefers philosophy to the Christian religion, wanting Plato canonized. He declares Savonarola's morality tedious and old-fashioned. Poliziano is contrasted with Pico de Mirandola, himself a philosopher and ruler of a small state. He protects Savonarola, admiring his convictions without sharing them. Where free-thinking is accepted as an ideology, he asserts, thinking in moral terms must also be allowed: 'morality is possible again' (*FA* III.1, 39; cf. *SL*.1, 258). At the end of the drama, Savonarola looks forward to his own short rule and his end.

At the beginning of the twentieth century, *Fiorenza* played with the struggle between modern amoral secularism and ideological movements: nationalism and socialism. While both promise to counter modern faithless amoralism, they soon misuse the power they had generated. Thomas Mann's sole play, unsuccessful on stage, did not receive much attention from readers either. But its discussion of modernity deserves more scrutiny in the twenty-first century.

A note of completion marks the end of the manuscript: 3 February 1905. Thomas married Katia Pringsheim on 11 February of that year. The marriage was to last until his death; it produced

Katia Mann with her children Erika and Klaus in Munich, *c.* 1907.

six children, and no serious marital disturbances are known. Katia soon grew into the task of protecting her husband's work by providing him with the feeling of security he dearly needed, especially at the beginning of their exile in 1933.

3
Two Loves and their Literary Outcomes

Near the end of 1899 Thomas Mann came into contact with the brothers Carl and Paul Ehrenberg. Carl, the younger one, took classes in composition at Dresden Conservatory. In Munich he often visited Paul, who studied painting at the Academy. Both brothers enjoyed getting together for music sessions with Thomas; Paul, an accomplished violinist, played first violin, Thomas the second and Carl accompanied both on the piano. Carl nurtured Thomas's love of Wagner by studying *Tristan und Isolde* with him. The friendship was most intense during the winters between 1900 and 1902; in the summers, Paul went to the Rhineland to practise *plein-air* painting with his teacher.

Paul was not one of the haughty artist outsiders of earlier acquaintances. He was more down to earth, but the relationship became problematic when Mann fell in love with him during the second winter of their friendship. In a letter to Grautoff of 22 February 1901 (*FA* XXI, 158–9), he expresses the passionate wish to dedicate a volume of novellas to Paul. Not that he regarded his new friend as an artist of his own intellectual stature: he needed to establish his superiority over Paul, as he had over Otto Grautoff.

After a stint in the military – Thomas Mann's feet, quite literally, did not tolerate the goose step and he was dismissed – he spent the first months of 1901 enjoying the carnival season and Munich's cultural life with the Ehrenbergs. But he was torn: as much as he enjoyed having friends and leaving his role as outsider behind, his erotic attraction to the heterosexual Paul disturbed his emotional balance. On 13 February 1901, he wrote to Heinrich that depression had led him to think of suicide, but his mood had changed to one of unexpected, pure, indescribable happiness (*FA* XXI, 154). The depression may have started with the discovery that strong homoerotic feelings were a permanent part of his adult sexuality. Although he had no intention of embarking on an actual homosexual relationship, the sentiments alone were of such disgrace at the time that he felt he had to be secretive. Still, the love experience itself was rewarding. Verses he had written into his notebook express joy over the realization that he was capable of real feelings of love, that the cold outsider stance he had assumed to be his as an author had not taken hold of him (*NB* II, 44, 46).

In late March or April 1901 the brothers must have told their friend about a murder in their home town of Leipzig. A well-to-do divorcée had shot a musician after he rejected her. Newspapers furnished Mann with more information, and soon he thought of applying the murder story to his experience with Paul Ehrenberg, perhaps as an episode in a society novel he had vaguely in mind. In July 1901 he added an idea about the woman's thoughts during the murder, together with a title for the planned novel: 'Die Geliebten' (The Beloved; *NB* I, 207). The title does not refer to couples in love with one another but to rejected lovers. In 1904 a new title, 'Maja', appears in the notebook, referring to the 'Veil of Maya' in Buddhism.

Ideas for characters in 'Die Geliebten' appear in Thomas Mann's notebooks of 1901. The murder victim is a professional violinist, modelled after Paul Ehrenberg and temporarily named 'P'. A woman, whose name – Adelaide – assonates with German *Leid*, and who is gifted with superior intelligence, loves him in vain and suffers. The model for her is Thomas Mann himself and his sister Julia. Since the Adelaide episode was to end with her murdering the violinist, most notes reflect Adelaide's negative experiences with 'P'. In real life, Mann's relationship with Paul remained more affable.

For a time, Thomas wanted to include allusions to Heinrich into the Adelaide affair. Adelaide is married to Albert, who, though a weakling, insists on praising the strong life. At the time, Heinrich was involved in writing the novel trilogy *Die Göttinnen* (1903; The Goddesses), whose female protagonist takes directions for her life from Nietzsche.

In May 1901 Thomas travelled to Florence again, this time in order to meet Heinrich and visit locations for his Savonarola project. In his short autobiography of 1930, he tells of a tender relationship with a Miss Mary Smith, an Englishwoman. He even claims that Mary and he had discussed marriage (*EK* III, 196). It was probably not much more than a flirt since he stayed in Florence for only about two weeks. Entries in a notebook indicate that he wrote letters to her for a while, but nothing has been preserved.

Mann's 'study' 'Die Hungernden' (1903; *DN*: The Starvelings; *SL* I: The Hungry) was written in May and June of 1902 under the impression – one could say under the pressure – of his futile love for Paul Ehrenberg. Although composed in the third person, the text is dominated by the single perspective of a man whose name, Detlef, brings to mind Detlev Spinell in 'Tristan'. Detlef tells himself: 'You are not permitted merely to exist, you must observe; you are not permitted to live, you must create; you are not permitted to love, you must know' (*FA* II.I, 376; cf. *DN*, 157). A writer must be an outsider. Departing from a dance hall, he leaves behind his beloved, who is attached to a friend, a painter obviously representing Paul Ehrenberg. Outside he observes an envious labourer with whom he identifies: 'We are brothers,' he tells himself (*FA* II.I, 379; cf. *DN*, 159). The story ends with a religious-sounding appeal for a loving humanity, one not excluding outsiders.

After finishing 'Die Hungernden' in June, Mann began writing his novella 'Tonio Kröger'. The thought of narrating the life of an outsider dated back to the late summer of 1899, when he had spent time in Denmark, a country that was home to Jens Peter Jacobsen, author of the melancholic novel *Niels Lyhne* (1880). Mann favoured the book's mood. His notebook of late 1899 echoes it: 'Tonio Kröger / Some by necessity lose their way, because there is no right path for them' (*NB* I, 175). Tonio Kröger, he adds in the next note, has a gentle temperament but is worn down by psychological perception ('psychologische Erkenntnis'). His psychological insights are tinged with Schopenhauer's pessimism. While the plan for 'Tonio Kröger' had started out in a melancholy mood, it developed into a more propitious one during the three-year gestation. The author found himself able to love.

Tonio, the son of an upright burgher, is an outsider by virtue of the artistic heritage of his beautiful, exotic and musically gifted mother. Her gift makes him different from his blonde and blue-eyed schoolmates. When he falls in love with one of them, Hans Hansen, Tonio's feelings are not returned, just as Thomas Mann's were not reciprocated by Paul Ehrenberg. Tonio's sense of being isolated is intensified when he cannot win the attention of Ingeborg Holm, a blonde and blue-eyed complement to Hans. He learns that love brings 'pain, distress and humiliation', that it obstructs the 'serenity required for forging something into a unified whole' (*FA* II.I, 255; cf. *DN*, 173–4). The creative talent belongs to the outsider, and to be an outsider is the artist's fate.

The centrally located fourth chapter in the novella registers Tonio's grievances in a conversation with his friend, the Russian painter Lisaveta. Although eager to be considered a modern author and prepared to accept the detachment from ordinary life essential for modern authors since Gustave Flaubert's *Madame Bovary*, Tonio yearns for love and human warmth, wanting a friend who is unlike the literati surrounding him. For the composition of this passage (*FA* II.I, 278; cf. *DN*, 193), Thomas Mann uses a note in which he praises 'P[aul] as his first and only "human" friend' who is different from his literary acquaintances (*NB* II, 72).

After so much bitterness, Tonio's subsequent confession to Lisaveta comes as a surprise: 'I love life' (*FA* II.I, 278; *DN*, 193). Summarizing his speech, she concludes: he has remained a burgher, a burgher on the wrong track. The judgement shakes Tonio's pride as an artist, but on the boat to Denmark he encounters the stormy, shapeless sea and experiences it as a symbol for the Whole of Being. The roar of wild animals – a polar bear and a Bengal tiger are stored in the ship's hold – reminds the reader of Schopenhauer's 'Will', but Tonio disregards thoughts of pessimism; the roaring fills him with enthusiasm for life in Nietzsche's sense. In Ålsgårde, at the Danish Baltic coast, the sea is beckoning and greeting him again (*FA* II.I, 303; *DN*, 215).

At the seaside hotel, Tonio Kröger encounters Hans Hansen and Ingeborg Holm, now morphed into two young Danes. As they reawaken Tonio's youthful love, the feeling of 'torpor, desolation, ice, intellect, and art' is offset (*FA* II.I, 315; cf. *DN*, 226). Mann uses words he had written in his notebook celebrating his love for Paul Ehrenberg (*NB* II, 46). In a letter to Lisaveta, still from Ålsgårde, Tonio acknowledges that his artistry is indeed that of an estranged burgher. His love of life, his love of ordinary people, provide for human warmth, goodness and humour in his writing and protect it from becoming artificial and lifeless. His is the love praised by St Paul (*FA* II.I, 318, cf. *DN*, 228).[1]

'Tonio Kröger' is a puzzling text, full of contradictions: Tonio will continue to write, now guided by his love of ordinary people, but reading fiction does not suit Hans Hansen's ordinary nature. Tonio devoted himself to artistic language, but his ancestors considered artists jugglers and they were not entirely wrong. 'Tonio Kröger' is a modern text: it plays with possibilities; it is meant to be ambiguous. The novella was published in *Neue deutsche Rundschau* in 1903 and in the same year in the volume of Mann's more recent stories, *Tristan*.

Heinrich sought to influence his younger brother when he sent him a copy of his short story 'Fulvia' (1904), a tale about the Italian

Risorgimento, the nineteenth-century struggle for Italian unity, for its freedom from Austrian domination and against Italian conservatism. The story was meant to persuade brother Thomas to write in a similar fashion to encourage the liberal movement in Wilhelminian Germany. Thomas answered in a letter, dated 27 February 1904, that his understanding of freedom equates the word 'freedom' with 'honesty'; some people call it his coldness. He is referring to his literary language that keeps itself free from religious or ideological attachments and does not aim at a certain political objective. Limitations to political freedom in a country were not necessarily detrimental to writers, he added; Russian literature had grown under massive political pressure. Freedom, Mann implies, is *within* the literature. When he writes in this letter, 'But I have no interest whatever in political freedom' (*FA* XXI, 269; *LR*, 64), he means the liberal parties of his day and their struggle for pecuniary interests.

But he opposed the power of the military in Wilhelminian Germany. The short story 'Ein Glück' (1904; literally 'a good fortune'; *SL* I, A Gleam) satirizes cavalry officers of nobility. The female protagonist, an outsider and officer's wife, echoes the feelings of the Adelaide character in the planned but unwritten novel 'Die Geliebten'. The degree of sarcasm and irony with which Mann treats militaristic Germany in this text proves that he did not subscribe to a conservative ideology.

The story 'Beim Propheten' (1904: *SL* I, At the Prophet's), of the same year, has an autobiographical backdrop: Mann had attended a reading of *Proclamations* by Ludwig Derleth, a Catholic bohemian and poet who imagined world conquest by a religious ruler. The event is narrated from the perspective of a 'novelist' who is one of the invited guests, similar to the author but with greater detachment from the bohemian environment. On the way out, the novelist engages an elegant lady in a conversation. She is modelled after Hedwig Pringsheim, the mother of Katia Pringsheim, whom Thomas

Mann was courting in 1904. The 'novelist', now easily recognized as the author, expresses his love for his soon-to-be wife.

Following their marriage ceremony Katia and Thomas Mann made a short wedding trip to Zurich and Lucerne. Once home, Mann wrote the essay 'Schwere Stunde' (1905; *DN*: Harsh Hour), celebrating the one-hundredth anniversary of Friedrich Schiller's death. The 'classical' dramatist and theorist of fiction was then of greater importance for German cultural life than he is today. The narrated monologue has Schiller wrestle with writer's block at night while working on his drama *Wallenstein*. Mann enlivens his text by combining details of Schiller's life and thoughts with memories of despair over his own writing. But he has Schiller collecting himself, regaining his ambition for greatness in the competition with Goethe, whom he loves with a 'yearning enmity' (*FA* 11.1, 421; cf. *DN*, 244). A visit to the room where his wife is sleeping brings comfort, and he reassures himself that he still loves her, but with a caveat: not completely. The fictive Schiller expresses the author's own worries when he reminds himself: 'On account of my mission, I am not permitted to be yours all too much' (*FA* 11.1, 427–8; cf. *DN*, 250–51). Mann's own seclusion was soon to be fixed to the morning hours when he regularly disappeared into his study to put pen to paper. Mann never used a typewriter.

In 1905 Thomas Mann's notebooks contained several ideas for future works. The theme of *Doktor Faustus* had been added to the project of a society novel where the Devil inspires a writer to produce great works (*NB* 11, 107, 121). Isolated notes indicate that he thought of a novel about Frederick 11 of Prussia, one about a confidence or con man, and a novella with the title 'Königliche Hoheit' (Royal Highness), which would become a full-length novel. Another idea for a novella enticed him even more: a non-Jew marrying into a wealthy Jewish family, a variant of what he had done himself. He knew that many of his contemporaries considered such marriages flawed, especially when a non-Jewish aristocrat married into a well-off Jewish family to restore solvency to his estate. Writing a story about such a marriage would make light of his own, providing distance in a playful manner. Soon he would write: 'If I have turned a thing into a sentence, what does the thing then still have to do with the sentence?' (FA XIV.I, 101).

The novella 'Wälsungenblut' (1906; The Blood of the Walsungs) is controversial for today's readers because it treats Jewish assimilation in Germany as a historic problem, using anti-Semitic clichés in the process. Nevertheless, it exists as one of Mann's best texts. It was printed in the January issue of *Die Neue Rundschau*, but before distribution the story was cut and replaced; Thomas Mann insisted that the type itself be destroyed. His father-in-law had complained. Katia's father, Alfred Pringsheim, was the son and heir of a Jewish entrepreneur who had become wealthy developing coal mines and railways in Upper Silesia. The son did not continue his father's business but became a distinguished Professor of Mathematics at the University of Munich. He did not practise the religion of his forebears, and also refused to convert to Christianity. His wife, Hedwig, came from a Protestant family; her great-grandfather had left the Jewish religion. The Pringsheim children were baptised. As a girl, Katia did not even know of her connection to Judaism.[2] Alfred Pringsheim built a house in Munich in an ornate style, decorated with antique and modern works of art.

'Wälsungenblut' introduces the Aarenholts, a wealthy Jewish family living in a mansion in Berlin's Tiergarten district. The description of their house exaggerates its opulence, mocking the lavish lifestyle of rich Berlin Jews. It was what Heinrich had done in his first novel, *Land of Cockaigne*. There are similarities between the Pringsheim family in Munich and the Aarenholts in Berlin, but also differences. The residence in Munich, although splendid, fell short of the imagined lavishness of the Aarenholt villa; Siegmund and Sieglinde Aarenholt are fraternal twins like Katia Pringsheim and her brother Klaus, but Madame Aarenholt and the two older

The Pringsheim family residence in Munich.

children differ from the corresponding members of the
Pringsheim family. Most important, the Pringsheims had
reached full assimilation, while the Aarenholts were still
striving to achieve it, placing Sieglinde under strain to marry
an unloved man. Siegmund is shown under pressure to outshine

Katia Pringsheim and her brother Klaus, Munich, *c.* 1900.

all others at the Wagner performance, taking hours to dress. He must show perfect assimilation.

Sieglinde's suitor, von Beckerath, is the caricature of a nobleman with the goal of marrying into money. He is 'of family', an aristocrat, but the reader meets a caricature: a 'short, canary-yellow, goateed, and zealously well-mannered' man (*FA* II.I, 431; *DN*, 257). The German expression for von Beckerath's zeal to please, *von eifriger Artigkeit*, has a later variant in '*von artiger Fügsamkeit*' (of well-mannered compliance; *FA* II.I, 435; cf. *DN*, 260). The word *artig* is almost exclusively applied to well-behaved children in German.

After von Beckerath has agreed that Siegmund and Sieglinde may visit Wagner's *The Valkyrie* by themselves for the last time, he disappears from the story. Siegmund's perspective prevails, when the twins are in the audience during the second part of the novella devoted to a performance of *The Valkyrie* (part two of *The Ring of the Nibelung*). Thomas Mann wanted to relate Jewish alienation to the alienation of the Volsungs in Wagner's music drama, where the first act presents the fugitive Siegmund lamenting his estrangement. His longing for community is always spurned; he is of a different kind than all the others (*FA* II.I, 451; cf. *DN*, 274). He and his twin sister, Sieglinde, are outsiders, despite being scions of the god Wotan.

Under the spell of Wagner's musical drama, Siegmund Aarenholt thinks for a moment of creating a 'work' (*FA* II.I, 456; *DN*, 278), of transforming the singularity of his feeling by expressing it artistically. But the wealthy heir's lifestyle prevents him from developing the passion needed for such a 'work'. Moreover, Siegmund's critical mind leads him to downgrade the theatrical performance on stage, making it appear unnatural and delusional. The electrical light glares in sudden effect, the singer playing Siegmund wears a wig, Sieglinde's full breasts heave, the character Hunding has a comical gait and a rusty voice, and it is contrived when the actors explain their fate in song (*FA* II.I, 449–54; cf. *DN*, 272–7).

After returning home, Siegmund and Sieglinde carry out the incest performed in Wagner's drama. Siegmund comments on the deed twice: in Mann's original conclusion and in an alternate one requested by the journal *Die Neue Rundschau*, whose editor wanted a less offensive ending. To Sieglinde's question about von Beckerath's future role, Siegmund replies in Mann's first version: 'Beganeft haben wir ihn, den Goy' (We betrayed him, the goy). *Beganeft* is Germanized Yiddish; *Ganef* means thief (*FA* II.II, 440). Both Siegmund and Sieglinde stole genuine love from the interloper. When Siegmund speaks these words, the marks of his Jewish origin stand out in his face: the twins have sealed their love as Jews. But their moment of authenticity is a fleeting one, as Sieglinde will still be married to von Beckerath for the sake of assimilation. The future appears in Siegmund's alternative answer: von Beckerath ought to be grateful because he will lead 'a less trivial existence from now on' (*DN*, 284). Dependent on Aarenholt money, he will have to tolerate his having been betrayed.

The theme of incest will appear again in *Der Erwählte* (1951; *The Holy Sinner*). 'Wälsungenblut' was issued in a private, limited printing in 1921, and in 1931 in French translation. The first public edition with the substitute ending appeared in 1958. The Frankfurt edition of 2004 restored the original wording (*FA* II.1, 463).

In 1906 Thomas began to write the novel *Königliche Hoheit* (1909; *Royal Highness*). Three years earlier, he had entered a verse by Pushkin into his notebook: 'You are Emperor (Czar), live alone!' and added: 'Motto for "Royal Highness"' (*NB* II, 86). He seemed to have had a tale about a lonely prince in mind for quite some time. Herman Bang's novella 'Her Highness' (in *Eccentric Stories*, 1886) had been a stimulus. Bang tells of a princess who leads an empty life, meant to be understood by the liberal Bang as a parody of monarchies. The theme of a lonely prince changed in 1904, the year of Mann's courtship with Katia. The prince was to be healed by marrying a commoner.

The novel portrays a small country governed by a constitutional monarchy. The grand duke reigns but does not govern, and the parliament always agrees to governmental necessities. The prime minister is a nobleman with a doctoral degree, a *Bildungsbürger*, who judges the courtiers with derision. The text of *Königliche Hoheit* mocks the feudal traditions but maintains a sense of highness as reflected in the title 'Royal Highness', an attitude validated by self-discipline. With this self-discipline, Prince Klaus Heinrich represents the dignity of his country, as the writer represents the world he has created on a different, 'higher' plane than that of everyday reality.

To show proper bearing while representing the dignity of the country is difficult for Prince Klaus Heinrich, who was born with a withered arm and hand. As in the case of Johannes Friedemann, the hunchback, Klaus Heinrich's deformed arm serves as a symbol of the personal aspect of Mann's outsider status: the need to hide the stigma of his homoerotic inclinations. Klaus Heinrich's birth defect is similar to that of Emperor Wilhelm II, but he does not resemble Wilhelm in any other respect. Perhaps Klaus Heinrich's modesty, together with his and his brother's, the reigning grand duke's, strict observance of the country's constitutional limits, was meant as a signal to the often unrestrained German emperor.

At the conclusion Prince Klaus Heinrich and Imma, the daughter of an American industrialist, plan to represent the dignity of their country jointly. The novel's message is that noble birth no longer determines personal rank, yet some people still surpass others in dignity. Klaus Heinrich and Imma endeavour to justify their elevated rank by studying economics, learning about the country's true problems. They desire to distinguish themselves from Klaus Heinrich's forebears, who tended to force wasteful expenditures on their subjects for the purpose of prestige. As a modernist, Thomas Mann questioned a rank achieved by noble birth, but he did believe in ranking established by personal authority, intelligence and willingness to serve the community.

Yet beyond the couple's happy end, we find the monarchy still in trouble: the billionaire father bought bonds that balance the budget, allowing for less austerity, but deficits are not curbed and productive investments seem absent. The monarchy, still on the path of bankruptcy, confirms that an agrarian duchy cannot maintain itself in the industrial age.

The novel resembles a Romantic fairy tale, although daughters of wealthy Americans did marry into British nobility. The allusions to fairy tales also serve as metaphors: Andersen's *Snow Queen* signifies the coldness of heart at court (*FA* IV.I, 63; cf. *RC*, 46, 'snow king'). When Klaus Heinrich and sister Ditlinde lose their way exploring the castle, they share Hansel and Gretel's fear (*FA* IV.I, 74; *RC*, 56). Imma's kiss on Klaus Heinrich's withered hand is a kiss of redemption similar to the kiss in *Sleeping Beauty* (*FA* IV.I, 313; *RC*, 264).

Mann added ambiguous playfulness to his theme about brothers. He made Prince Klaus Heinrich the second-born son of the previous grand duke. When Albrecht, the first-born son, becomes grand duke, he delegates most of his public appearances to his younger, more popular brother, alluding to brother Thomas's greater success with his books. Heinrich appreciated the modernity of the novel (*FA* XXI, 437–9) but was offended, calling it an 'attack' (*FA* XXII, 710; *LR*, 124).

When a reviewer found modernist, even democratic, tendencies in the novel, Thomas was satisfied, although he refused to acknowledge that he had advocated democracy (*FA* XXI, 437–9). A realistic touch is added by the end of Doctor Überbein, who supported Prince Klaus Heinrich's sense of aristocratic highness and seemed to be an example of how disadvantaged people could achieve a higher rank by ambition and self-discipline. Having come from extreme poverty, Überbein's extraordinary energy enabled him to reach the level of instructor in a Gymnasium. But his ambition destroys him. His name, Überbein, can be read as an allusive critique of Nietzsche's concept of *Übermensch*, his imagined objective for a developing mankind. *Königliche Hoheit* appeared in instalments in the journal *Die Neue Rundschau* from January to September 1908 and appeared as a book in October 1909.

The relationship with brother Heinrich had been cool for a long time. Its nadir was Thomas's aggressive letter of 5 December 1903, criticizing Heinrich's novel *Die Jagd nach Liebe* and his novel trilogy *Die Göttinnen*. He blamed his brother for using sexual scenes in a trivial manner. But on 22 October 1905, Heinrich wrote a letter (not preserved) praising *Fiorenza*, moving Thomas to tears (*FA* XXI, 330; *LR*, 73). Heinrich fictionalized worries about his brother in the short story 'Abdankung' (Abdication), written in November 1905 and published in *Simplicissimus* in January of the following year. He dedicated it to 'my brother Thomas'.[3] Thomas thanked him in a letter, praising the piece and assuring him that it almost felt as if he had written it himself (*FA* XXI, 346; *LR*, 79). He probably meant to signal that he had understood its intimate message. 'Abdankung' tells of Felix, a gifted student, who enjoys dominating his ordinary classmates until he suddenly submits to one of them. When he persuades his new master to command him to go down to the fish in the pond, Felix complies and drowns. Heinrich seems

Thomas Mann with the actors before the performance of *Fiorenza* in Lübeck, 1925.

to warn Thomas against Tonio Kröger's love for ordinary people. Also, homoerotic desire appears as a sickness in Heinrich's story. The name Felix for the protagonist in 'Abdankung', meaning 'the happy one' in Latin, may have been an ironic play on Thomas's success.

During the early twentieth century, writers were often asked by newspapers and magazines to answer questions of general cultural interest. One such survey asked about the cultural value of the theatre. The question triggered Mann's 1908 essay 'Versuch über das Theater' (Essay on the Theatre; *FA* XIV.I, 123–73), where he outlined much of his position on German culture. City theatres, *Stadttheaters*, were centres of bourgeois culture in Germany. Mann considered the civic theatre as a kind of temple that might eventually replace religious institutions. But he also argued against the superior ranking of drama among the arts, including Richard Wagner's musical dramas. The multi-dimensional novel, he insists, deserves higher prestige in modernity.

4

'Death in Venice', the First World War and *The Magic Mountain*

In 1910 Thomas Mann put aside an entire notebook filled exclusively with notes for a novel on Frederick II of Prussia; he had decided to begin *Bekenntnisse des Hochstaplers Felix Krull* (1954; Confessions of Felix Krull, Confidence Man) instead. Inspired by a Romanian impostor's popular autobiography, the new book was meant to showcase the upper reaches of fashionable society from the perspective of a confidence man. Since it would also contain autobiographical material from the author's own life, the novel had the potential of becoming a parody of autobiography itself, with Goethe's *Poetry and Truth* in mind. But it must have been difficult for Mann combining the ill-educated Romanian's commonplace language with phrases natural to an educated German who had read his Goethe, since that was Krull's ambition. Interrupting the toil by writing a short story could offer relief.

Mann found a topic sometime in May or June 1911, when he, his wife Katia and his brother Heinrich spent time at the Adriatic Sea. While briefly visiting a hotel on the Lido of Venice, Mann was struck by the beauty of a fourteen-year-old boy. Katia noticed his fascination but probably had accepted her husband's bisexual feelings by then.[1] More worrisome must have been Heinrich's awareness. But the stay on the Lido lasted only a few days; a cholera epidemic drove the Mann party away.

Although he soon thought of transforming his emotional experience with the boy into a narrative text, Mann could not openly narrate his fascination with the boy. Contemporary social censure of homosexuality made him look for camouflage. The thought of retelling Goethe's love story of 1823 with the nineteen-year-old Ulrike von Levetzow in Marienbad (Mariánské Lázně, now Czech Republic), and his loss of dignity over the rejection, came to mind. But Goethe's marriage plans were too far removed from the feelings occupying him. Mann needed to tell how it felt to encounter a forbidden desire while having to condemn it, and he needed to get it across to his brother, meaning that he had to be recognizable in his protagonist Gustav von Aschenbach but in an image distorted enough to serve as camouflage for others.

Aschenbach therefore became a much older writer whose works were esteemed by the educational authorities. But these works were Mann's abandoned plans that Heinrich, familiar with the development of his brother, could easily recognize. More so: when the narrator describes recurring themes of Aschenbach's works, readers familiar with Mann's style could make out characters from his published works. When describing Aschenbach's journey to Venice and recording the progress from attraction to passionate love for the pubescent boy Tadzio, the narrator uses his protagonist's point of view, but he also signals distance. He calls Aschenbach 'ageing', 'confused', even an 'infatuated fool' (*der Betörte*; FA II.I, 566; DN, 344). In a small square in the city, after eating contaminated strawberries, Aschenbach blames himself for his homoerotic passion in an interior monologue reminiscent of a Platonic dialogue.

But 'Der Tod in Venedig' contains another narrative, beginning with a traveller emerging from the chapel at the Munich Northern Cemetery. He resembles the Greek god Hermes, the messenger of the gods, a god of relations and transitions, of life and death. The narrator does not recognize the Greek god, a mere Bavarian traveller to him, nor does he acknowledge other messengers guiding Aschenbach to the Lido. One, disguised as an unlicensed gondolier, is Charon, who ferries his passenger to his place of death. Aschenbach's joy on the Lido is expressed in elements of Greek culture, which allowed for homoerotic love. Poetic inventions in the style of Plato's dialogue 'Phaidon' join the idea of beauty to passion, until those images are contradicted by a Dionysian dream with a cruel orgy of humans and animals under a wooden phallus.

On his last day Aschenbach observes his beloved from the beach, as Tadzio walks into the 'hazy-boundless' sea (*das Nebelhaft-Grenzenlose*; *FA* II.1, 592; cf. *DN*, 366). When the boy turns around looking towards his admirer, smiling, beckoning him to follow, Aschenbach perceives him as Hermes Psychagogos, the guide of his soul, promising him freedom in the sea as a symbol of the indestructible 'Will', the Whole of Being. The last paragraph belongs to the biographer, who does not know of Aschenbach's liberation. 'Der Tod in Venedig' was published in 1912 in the October and November issues of *Die Neue Rundschau*. It came out as a book in February 1913.

There are references to the period's political tensions in the text: when Aschenbach's boat arrives in Venice, young Italian-speaking passengers from the town of Pola, then belonging to the Austro-Hungarian Empire (now the Croatian town of Pula), cheer exercising Italian troops; the Polish boy Tadzio hates a Russian family. Among the root causes of the coming First World War were fears by political elites of both Austria-Hungary and Russia that their country's status as a great imperial power was threatened by discontented populations within their borders who harboured their own nationalistic ambitions.

Heinrich wrote a strange review of the novella in the liberal magazine *März* in March 1913.[2] He describes its action as the depiction of a literary master's ensnarement by the beauty of a diseased city, standing in for Wilhelminian Germany. Written as if his brother had joined Heinrich's opposition to imperial Germany, the novella seems to predict the fall of an empire, much like Émile Zola's Rougon-Macquart novels.[3]

Heinrich was not the only one predicting war. Germany felt threatened by the French–Russian alliance of 1894, fearing possible conflict on two fronts. Alliance with Great Britain could have eased the threat, but Germany's move to check British naval power with the construction of a fleet of battleships, starting in 1898, eliminated this option. This imprudent policy, favoured and pushed by Kaiser Wilhelm, Queen Victoria's grandson, forced Britain to enter a naval arms race and to join in the Triple Entente with France and Russia. Germany's only reliable ally, the Austro-Hungarian Empire, competed with Russia for influence in the Balkans. Austria-Hungary's attack on Serbia as punishment for the assassination of Franz Ferdinand, the designated heir of the imperial throne, started a war that soon lost all political sense when it degenerated into the desire to win at all cost.

In late summer 1913 Thomas Mann interrupted *Bekenntnisse des Hochstaplers Felix Krull* for a novella he called a humorous counterpart to 'Death in Venice' (*FA* XXI, 527). It was destined to grow into the novel *Der Zauberberg* (1924; *The Magic Mountain*). Its setting, a sanatorium in the Alps, had offered itself in the spring of 1912 when Thomas visited Katia in Davos, where she was taking treatments.

In a letter to Heinrich, written 8 November 1913, Mann finds less humour in his undertaking. He could not orient himself in the world, as Heinrich had managed to do, he lamented; an inborn 'sympathy with death' was growing in him, together with an apprehension about the condition of the world and the country: 'It is awful to be weighed down by the whole misery of the times and the fatherland without the strength to lend it form' (*FA* XXI, 535; cf. *LR*, 119). But the seeming writer's block stopped him only temporarily; for months, he made steady progress on *Der Zauberberg*. His expression 'sympathy with death', overshadowing the novel, appears in this letter to Heinrich for the first time. Since in death all connections to the world cease, contemplating it can be liberating for the inventive writer. But death is also a reminder of the end

Katia Mann in the Sanatorium at Oberstdorf in 1920.

of life and all its accomplishments. 'Sympathy with death' is an ambivalent formula.

When war broke out in August 1914, Thomas Mann, together with most Germans, was convinced that his country was threatened by Russia's mobilization. Surrounded by hostile nations, it needed to break out of its encirclement. At first he judged the war, quite correctly, as a catastrophe (*FA* XXII, 38). But the enthusiastic response of Germany's citizens, eager to defend their country, soon thrilled him, and he supported the common goal with his war essays. The dissimilar reactions to the war by the Mann brothers brought the lingering mistrust between them to an open conflict, and they communicated only through their publications. An attempt at reconciliation launched by Heinrich on 30 December 1917 did not succeed. Rapprochement had to wait until 1922; even then relations remained fragile.

The war enthusiast was spared active duty. Several of Thomas's war publications speak about the trenches as the only honourable place to be, but he was convinced that his nerves would fail him, opting to serve with his pen instead. One of his essays, 'Gedanken im Kriege' (Thoughts in War), published in *Die Neue Rundschau* in November 1914, argues against the Allies' war objectives: to save civilization by beating German militarism. He takes the position that culture is of a higher order than civilization and is compatible with art and war. Mann's war essays are embarrassing for contemporary readers; they soon embarrassed him as well, and he excused them in letters to friends as 'bottomless journalistic' (*FA* XXII, 44).

In 'Friedrich und die grosse Koalition' (1914; Frederick the Great and the Grand Coalition), Mann used material from his research on the Prussian king's life. Frederick had opened the Seven Years' War with the invasion of Saxony, presented by Mann now as a historic necessity comparable to the German invasion of Belgium. He hoped that history would repeat itself and let Germany emerge from the war unscathed, but worrisome undertones are recognizable.

In his answer to a survey question by a Swedish newspaper ('An die Redaktion von Svenska Dagbladet'; 'To the Editor of Svenska Dagbladet') on how cultural relations between the warring nations could be restored, Mann complained angrily about the war propaganda by Germany's enemies. Although no longer expecting a German victory by May 1915, he asserted that the country would put all its energy into the restitution of its power should it be humiliated. The prediction turned out to be only too true.

Mann's war essay, *Betrachtungen eines Unpolitischen* (1918, *Reflections of a Nonpolitical Man*), makes for difficult reading. Overall, the deliberations lack the lucidity of his narrative prose. The intent can be understood best as a long answer to Heinrich's invitation to devote his writings to propaganda for a more democratic Germany. Freedom from political engagement for his writing defines 'non-political' for Thomas: 'Freedom, duty and freedom again, that is Germany,' he writes (*FA* XIII.I, 305; *RM*, 202).

While Heinrich had aligned himself with the French Republic and its partisan politics, Thomas regarded French democracy as a plutocracy governing a people with enthusiasm for prosperity (*FA* XIII.I, 263; *RM*, 174), a quality he had depicted unfavourably in *Buddenbrooks*. He saw democracy merely as a struggle for power. Although the Mann brothers' Germany was a constitutional monarchy with a legislature, parliament and partisan politics, the German *Bildungsbürger* held on to the idea of a benevolent and autonomous prime minister supported by the monarch, a system that he also credited with Germany's social progress (*FA* XIII.I, 285; *RM*, 188). He did suggest change: intelligence (*Geist*) and power should cooperate in a *Volksstaat* (people's state), designating the minority *Bildungsbürger* as preferred rulers. There was one progressive feature; Thomas advocated educational privileges enjoyed by the wealthy to be revoked (*FA* XIII.I, 282; *RM*, 187).

Among the contradictions in *Betrachtungen*, the one about nationalism is characteristic: his claim that Germany can be both national and transnational because of its history. German tribes had managed to maintain their special characteristics by resisting the Roman Empire, Mann writes. Later, they rebelled against the Roman Church and against Napoleon's Europe. But the same Germany, looking east as well as west from Europe's middle, also thinks in cosmopolitan terms. The unpolitical man can see the war as a 'strife between European brothers' (*FA* XIII.I, 52; cf. *RM*, 29).

Thomas directed much hostility towards German sympathizers of French civilization who opposed the country's war effort. He called them *Zivilisationsliteraten*, literati for 'civilization', the prime *Zivilisationsliterat* being his brother Heinrich. In the voice of Zola, who had attacked French military authorities, Heinrich Mann had condemned the supporters of the war in Germany, meaning especially his brother without naming him: 'Striving to become national poet for just half a generation, in case there is enough breath left, but always going with the flow, always cheerleading,

In this postcard to Maximilian Brantl, sent on 18 June 1916, Mann apologizes for his pencil marks in Heinrich Mann's *Zola*.

mad with enthusiasm, without feelings of responsibility for the growing catastrophe, even ignorant about it, like the rest of them'. A conformist writer 'with all his gifts is scarcely more than an entertaining parasite'.[4] Heinrich's essay 'Zola' was published in November 1915. Thomas, deeply offended, answered in *Betrachtungen eines Unpolitischen*. He finished the book in March 1918; it appeared in October, a few weeks before the end of the war. After finishing the essay, with the war still under way, Mann penned the idyllic autobiographical story 'Herr und Hund' (1919; A Man and his Dog). It contains landscape descriptions, unusual for him.

We can find Mann's reactions to the loss of the war in the diaries that cover the time span between 11 September 1918 and 1 December 1921.[5] On hearing that the German high command found it necessary to end the war, he writes on 5 October 1918: 'The catastrophe has come and with it the global defeat of a German conservative way of thinking.' On 9 November, one day after the diary records the shocking news of the conditions for the armistice, the entries reflect a more positive mood; the diarist now no longer objects to a German republic, and he does not bemoan the abdication of Kaiser Wilhelm nor the demise of the other German monarchies.[6]

A socialist revolution broke out in Bavaria on 8 November 1918, followed, a day later, by the declaration of a German republic in Berlin led by social democrats. Asked to declare his support in favour of the revolution, Thomas complied. The nation, he wrote, feels carried by the energy of the future, as it did in 1914. He voted for democratic middle-class parties in the elections of 1919.[7] He has some sympathy for the social aims of the anarchistic, non-Marxist author Gustav Landauer in his *For Socialism* (1911), while meeting the book's utopian features with scepticism; it was similar with a source about a medieval world view and its pre-capitalistic economic order that served him in preparing for the continuation of *Der Zauberberg*.[8] The Bavarian Republic developed more radical features; the Council Republic (Räterepublik, after the Russian Soviets) turned Communist in 1919. The diary now contains fear that his house might be expropriated or that proletarian bands might loot it.

An idyllic relationship with his six-month-old daughter Elisabeth helped offset Mann's fears and disappointments. On 2 November 1918, a few days before the beginning of the Bavarian revolution, he started an outline for a poem in hexameter about the child. But he did not turn away from the world. On 21 December 1918, the diary records his first insights into the 'stupid' (*hirnverbrannt*) failure of Germany's foreign policy before the war.

Towards the end of April 1919, Katia gave birth to the couple's sixth child, Michael. During the first days of May, Munich's Council Republic fell to federal troops after bourgeois hostages were killed. This outrage was disturbing to Mann, but a month later he signed an appeal for a policy of reconciliation directed at the restituted Bavarian government and helped to defend Ernst Toller, a dramatist who had played a role in the Council Republic.[9] Toller's life was spared.

On 19 January 1920, Mann envisioned a union of conservatism (the *Bildungsbürger*) and socialism for Germany rather than a parliamentary democracy. At the same time, the National Socialist Workers' Party was formed in Munich with Adolf Hitler as its main speaker, demanding a socialism limited to the nation state and opposing international Marxism. What distinguished the party platform from Thomas Mann's imaginings was its rabidly anti-Semitic message. Mann protested the 'Hakenkreuz-Unfug' (swastika nuisance) in 1921 (*FA* XV.I, 436) and soon began to moderate his misgivings about the word 'democracy'. He retained the idea of socialism, even in the totalitarian form of Russian Bolshevism, as a possible 'corrective' to bourgeois democracy.[10] But he avoided being taken as a 'party activist' (*Parteimensch*; *FA* XXIII.I, 350).

Three months later, Mann composed *Vorsatz* (meaning both foreword and intention), as he continued *Der Zauberberg*, promising a story from the 'deepest past'. The second chapter, addressing Hans Castorp's youth and choice of profession, describes the social conditions of the pre-war era – often seen with nostalgia as la belle époque, or gilded age – as something negative. The narrator accuses the period of failing to answer the question of meaning (*FA* v.I, 54; cf. *MW*, 37), much as Mann himself had done in his letter to Heinrich on 8 November 1913, where he lamented the 'misery of the time' with its lack of guidance.

Hans Castorp's seclusion in the sanatorium alludes to the Romantic myth of the minstrel knight Tannhäuser, who lives in a cave under a mountain with Venus, longing to be free. References to Wagner's opera appear occasionally in the novel. In reverse, Castorp finds freedom while secluded in the sanatorium. Like many of his generation, he had been unable to settle on a lasting goal for himself during his adolescence; now he can engage in a search for a true purpose in life. His fellow patients, by contrast, waste their time with frivolous activities that will finally dominate them, as the society at the sanatorium Berghof slides into decay.

The liberty Hans Castorp enjoys parodies the writer's freedom Mann claims for himself. It was the point of contention with his brother, who had committed himself to political engagement. In the sanatorium, the brotherly opposition is represented by the Italian humanist Lodovico Settembrini, determined to teach Castorp an enlightened rational ideology. Although Settembrini does so with conviction, his advanced tuberculosis casts a negative light on his effort, for both the protagonist and the reader. Moreover, Hans is distracted; he has fallen in love with Clawdia Chauchat, a Russian woman whose features enliven one of his old memories: the object of a one-sided homoerotic infatuation with a fellow student. Hetero- and homoerotic love, the thought of death and his strong sense of freedom make Hans Castorp a German Romantic resisting Western ideology.

Despite having planned a short visit, Castorp is delighted when the chief physician discovers a slight shadow on his lung, justifying more time at the sanatorium. He uses it to observe a host of international patients being treated, as the book partially turns into a society novel. A critical picture of pre-war Europe emerges. Hans Castorp eventually wins the exotic Russian lady with his declaration of love in French, while invoking his Romantic idea of an ambivalent unity of body, sex and death.

Clawdia leaves the day after the intimate encounter. When she returns, she is accompanied by the coffee king, Mynheer Peeperkorn. But rather than surrendering to jealousy, Castorp transcends his desire, transforming it into a loving alliance with Clawdia in favour of Peeperkorn, whose death they both fear (*FA* v.1, 906–7; *MW*, 712). Love is humanized in this alliance. Talking to Clawdia, Hans calls death the 'genial principle' capable of generating a new appreciation of life and humanity (*FA* v.1, 903; *MW*, 709). His vision of death still meets Schopenhauer's precepts: life and love must be seen against the background of a separation from all bonds, of the 'Will', which is both nothingness and the source of all being.

With Clawdia absent, a new antagonist challenges Settembrini's liberalism and Enlightenment ideology. He is Leo Naphta, born in a *shtetl* and trained in Jesuit schools after his conversion to Catholicism. Naphta positions the medieval economy in opposition to pernicious capitalism, while offering a corrective in a communism under God established by terror (*FA* v.1, 604–9; *MW*, 474–8). Although Mann had the opportunity to observe a model for Naphta's stringent rhetoric when he met the Hungarian Marxist György Lukács, Naphta's arguments do not mirror Lukács's Marxism.[11] With Naphta, Thomas Mann makes a political statement: socialist ideologies can become as doctrinaire as religious ones and can turn to terror as an instrument for maintaining power.

Naphta's as well as Settembrini's influence are neutralized by Mynheer Peeperkorn, whose domineering personality celebrates the cult of 'life'. Such a movement, not unlike a substitute religion, had originated in pre-war literature in the wake of Nietzsche's philosophy. Peeperkorn stages himself as Bacchus or Dionysus and plays with Christian imagery, both imitating and mocking it:

On holiday with Gerhart Hauptmann (centre) and family at Kloster, Hiddensee, 1924.

when he observes an eagle, he sympathizes with the raptor striking a lamb, killing the Christian symbol. But he can also imitate the voice of Jesus in Gethsemane or carry his head tilted as if nailed to the cross. The martyr may suddenly change into a pagan priest, invoking 'the sacrament of lust' (*FA* v.i, 894; *MW*, 702). Sensing a rival for Clawdia's affection in Hans Castorp, Peeperkorn proclaims his creed of 'life': 'life' is potency; its loss is defeat, a sin for which there is no mercy, no forgiveness (*FA* v.i, 855; *MW*, 672). When he actually loses his potency, he commits suicide; the cult of life has contradicted itself. The Peeperkorn episode satirizes the tendency to establish substitute religions. In Peeperkorn, Mann portrayed many of the mannerisms of Gerhart Hauptmann, then considered Germany's greatest writer. Recognizing the parody, Hauptmann was understandably annoyed. But with a good letter, the author managed to ease his rival's anger (*FA* XXIII.i, 143).

Hans Castorp believes he has found an answer to life's contradictions in a dream during a ski excursion, where he has fallen asleep in the snow. Waking up, he reflects on the joyful, as well as horrifying, images of human activity he has seen in his dream and concludes that human beings must live with these contradictions. God or the Devil, good or evil, death or life, spirit or nature are no more than complements for *homo dei*, the 'man of God', whom God has placed in the middle. With this insight in mind, Castorp pledges that for the 'sake of goodness and love, man shall not grant death dominion over his thoughts' (*FA* v.I, 747–8; cf. *MW*, 587–8). The nihilistic freedom involved in the focus on death should give way to kindness and charity. But this insight bypasses the novel's action; it is a message to the reader, as Castorp forgets his pledge and remains in the cloistered environment of the sanatorium.

In August 1914 Thomas had decided to let *Der Zauberberg* end with the outbreak of the war.[12] Still confident about the outcome, he likely expected a changed environment after the war ended: German influence would end money-driven economies in Europe. Hans Castorp would use his freedom in the sanatorium to discover a new social orientation. But such prospects had vanished by 1923 and 1924 when Mann wrote the concluding chapters. Castorp has forgotten his dream, and love, as a socially determining factor, emerges only as a question in the novel's final sentence, asking whether love will be able to rise from the 'world festival of death' (*FA* v.I, 1085; *MW*, 854).

At the end of the sub-chapter 'Fülle des Wohllauts' (Fullness of Harmony), the narrator, focusing mostly on the reader, debates the *lied* of the linden tree, one of Castorp's favourite recordings. It is a song of Romantic nationalism, one of the causes of the war that must now be abandoned, as Nietzsche had abandoned Wagner's music in spite of loving it. The future belongs to the idea of a new love, carried on Nietzsche's lips when he dies, though he could not utter it (*FA* v.I, 989–90; *MW*, 643).[13] Hans Castorp, storming ahead on the battlefield in the final scene, still sings his *lied*; he is still fighting for Romantic nationalism and may die for it. In 1924, when the last pages of *Der Zauberberg* were written, the 'new love' expresses itself in socialism and in European cooperation.

5

The Weimar Republic and
Two *Joseph* Novels

Thomas Mann was delighted when he learned from Ernst Robert
Curtius, a German professor of Romance languages, that there
were reformist moves underway in France with goals similar to what
he himself had in mind. Mann's essay 'Das Problem der deutsch–
französischen Beziehungen' (1922; The Problem of German–French
Relations) welcomed French writers, like André Gide, willing to
improve German–French cultural interaction. Gide's, as well as
Curtius's, internationalism was quite antagonistic to the passionate
nationalism that had gripped post-war France and Germany.

In this spirit, Mann gladly accepted an invitation from his
home town of Lübeck to contribute to a 'Nordic Week' designed
to encourage contacts between Germany and the Scandinavian
countries. He called his lecture 'Goethe und Tolstoi' (1922; Goethe
and Tolstoy), showing that despite all their differences, both writers
shared a lively interest in education and a concern for humanity,
Humanität in German. Thomas Mann began using this word now
as a substitute for 'democracy' when he wished to describe the less
materialistic form of organized society he hoped would develop
in Germany. He repeated the lecture in several cities and countries,
enjoying the contact with his audience, whether speaking or reading
from his works.

Many Germans, unable to come to terms with the loss of the war,
blamed the capitulation on socialist Jews; anti-Semitism increased.
The successful author Jakob Wassermann complained in his

Thomas Mann at his desk, Munich, 1922.

autobiographical book *Mein Weg als Deutscher und Jude* (1921;
My Life as German and Jew, 1933) about the relentless anti-Semitic
hostility he encountered, more so because he regarded himself
as a 'German Jew' rather than a 'Jewish Jew'. It was a justified
assertion: not only had his family lived in Germany for generations,
but his writing was centred on German or German-Jewish themes.
Mann reminded his friend that his success alone made him an
outsider, as happened to all good writers in cosmopolitan Germany
(*GW* XIII, 463–5). It was not something Wassermann accepted:
Thomas Mann could hardly understand, what it meant to have
one's origin constantly degraded (*GW* XIII, 887–9).

In January 1922 Heinrich Mann suffered from several life-
threatening ailments. Thomas sent flowers and heartfelt wishes,
expressing his desire for a reconciliation should Heinrich share
his sentiment (*FA* XXII, 422–3). The restored relationship became
cordial in public but remained frail.

The government of the new German Republic never won full
support from its *Bildungsbürger* class. The first Reichspräsident,

Jakob Wassermann, Thomas Mann and Samuel Fischer in St Moritz, Switzerland, 1931.

Friedrich Ebert, leader of the Social Democratic Party between 1913 and 1919, who had been instrumental in establishing order during the revolution, received little credit. When the republic's founding parties lost their majority in the election of 1920, it was a setback never to be reversed. Thomas Mann had met President Ebert in 1922 during a Goethe celebration in Frankfurt am Main; he appreciated his unassuming dignity.

The peace treaty of Versailles obliged Germany to pay reparations for the destruction caused by the war; France needed these funds to repay American war loans and threatened to occupy the industrial region of the Ruhr to collect coal supplies by force. In 1921 a

Thomas Mann (right) with his brother Heinrich in Berlin, 1927.

three-party coalition – Centrum (Catholic), Social Democrats and a left-liberal party – managed to stall the occupation of the Ruhr temporarily. As Minister of Foreign Affairs, Walther Rathenau – one of the founders of the left-liberal party – won an opening for beleaguered Germany in the following year by concluding a treaty in Rapallo, Italy, with Communist Russia. Rathenau came from a Jewish family of industrialists. He considered himself completely German, but nationalists could not tolerate a Jew as a political leader. A terrorist organization assassinated him.

When Mann read about Rathenau's murder, he decided to turn an essay devoted to dramatist Gerhart Hauptmann's sixtieth birthday into a speech for university students, hoping to win their support for the new republic. The essay, under the title 'Von deutscher Republik' (1922; The German Republic), addresses Hauptmann as 'king of the republic'. Hauptmann had been a supporter of the constitution. The idea of combining an appreciation for him with an address to students suggests that Thomas envisioned writers taking the place of former royalty, giving needed direction to the nation.

With the occupation of the Ruhr in 1923, the German currency collapsed. In the midst of runaway inflation, when materials and food were scarce, Thomas Mann, a lifelong pessimist, nevertheless tried to conjure up the prospect of a positive future for his country. In articles for the American magazine *Current History*, he assures his readers that Germany's intellectuals were willing to shoulder active politics as part of their destiny, exactly what *Betrachtungen eines Unpolitischen* had so passionately rejected. While attributing the rise of totalitarian movements in Germany to France's harsh policies, he assures his readers that those movements have no future. In letters to the American journal *The Dial*, Mann complains about the apathy of the world watching the imminent breakdown of Germany, a consequence of French demands for reparations that the country could not pay. Such a policy is tolerated, he alleges, because of the lingering harm caused by the Allied war propaganda, which had labelled Germans Huns and barbarians deserving of harsh treatment.

But, Thomas Mann's public role expanded. The PEN club organized a dinner in his honour in London in 1924, where he met George Bernard Shaw, John Galsworthy and H. G. Wells. At home, he became controversial: 'Von deutscher Republik' had alienated him from many of the nationalistically inclined *Bildungsbürger*. Hostility grew between him and the leading Munich newspaper *Münchener Neueste Nachrichten*, once a liberal publication. In 1924, in an article celebrating the sixtieth birthday of the writer Ricarda Huch, Mann argued against the distinction between an inspired author (*Dichter*) and a prose writer (*Schriftsteller*). Conservatives had questioned the prose writer's representative role in German culture, denying him the ability to lead creatively, as the essay 'Goethe und Tolstoi' had envisioned. Thomas Mann's dismissal of the *Zivilisationsliterat* had come back to haunt him.

Agreeing with the cultural philosophy of the theologian Ernst Troeltsch, Mann now considered the Romantic turn against the ideology of the French Revolution a German error (*FA* XV.I, 723–6; *PL*, 141–6), but he still wanted Nietzsche to lead (*FA* XV.I, 791). He regarded National Socialism, Adolf Hitler's movement, as a Romantic phenomenon. Romantic, indeed, was its idea that the highly industrialized and entrepreneurial German nation consisted of a people of peasants and that the country needed more agricultural land. Its tendency to have Germany organized as a totalitarian state was not Romantic at all.

A new essay volume received the title *Bemühungen* (1925; literally 'efforts': the word replaces 'essays'). Its main component is a much enlarged version of 'Goethe und Tolstoi' with additions opposing Bolshevism and condemning German fascism. Thomas Mann calls the Social Democratic Party Germany's true national party, expressing his hope that the representatives of the working population would align themselves with the *Bildungsbürger*. Most upper-class and middle-class German voters did not share Mann's political preference. In the essay 'Die Ehe im Übergang' (1925; Marriage in Transition), Mann declares homoerotic love to be Romantic aestheticism because it does not contribute to 'life'. Marriage, by contrast, grounded in fidelity, is justified by the social order and thus by 'life'. The essay was motivated by Thomas Mann's opposition to fascist Romanticism; it has an element of self-negation.

The story 'Unordnung und frühes Leid' (1925; Disorder and Early Sorrow), set in 1923 when Germany's inflation was rampant, mirrors the difficulty of Mann's decision to disengage from the Schopenhauerian idea of timelessness and think in terms of progress. The family story has an autobiographical base. The father, a self-portrait in the role of a professor of history, is preparing a lecture on the Glorious Revolution in Britain. He will contrast William III's progressiveness with Philip II of Spain's futile struggle against modernity. While he loves Philip's noblesse, he will condemn his fight. His own persistent Romanticism is betrayed by his preference for his youngest child, his five-year-old daughter. On a lonely walk at night, he admits to himself that his intense attachment to this child is really no more than an escape from the present, represented by his older children. Yet his beloved little daughter becomes enamoured with a guest of her much older siblings, a student. The professor is forced to recognize for himself, and for his author, that he cannot live outside of the flow of time.

When Mann wrote the story in 1925, the Dawes Plan had begun to solve the reparations crisis. British and American pressure on France forced the French government to end the Ruhr occupation. The mark was stabilized but 'disorder' remained a threat. 'Unordnung und frühes Leid' is a document of the German people's fear of a return to an unstable currency and further pressures by France. This fear hung over the German republic and helped to cause its end. Fear of a destructive inflation is still a factor in German politics.

On the occasion of Thomas Mann's fiftieth birthday in June 1925, the city of Munich staged a splendid celebration in its city hall. In thanking everyone, Mann remarked that he had come to realize, late in his life, that all works of art of any value are conceived and received in a social context.

In January 1926 he accepted an invitation by the Paris branch of the Carnegie Foundation for International Peace to deliver a speech in Paris. The recently negotiated treaties of Locarno, which had eased the hostilities between France and Germany, provided the political context. The lecture in Paris expressed Mann's conviction that intellectuals in both nations can and should exert influence over the political climate controlling their nations. He assured his French colleagues of an increased commitment to the idea of democracy among the German people, a more hopeful than realistic assessment. A detailed narrative report of his nine days in Paris can be found in 'Pariser Rechenschaft' (1926; Parisian Account). In an aside, unrelated to the argument, he upbraids Alfred Baeumler's essay on Johann Jakob Bachofen as guided by conservative ideology and

Thomas and Katia Mann with their two youngest children in Kampen, Sylt, 1927.

Annual Meeting of the Sektion für Dichtkunst, Berlin, October 1929.

therefore unsuited for the politics of the time. We will hear more
about Bachofen in connection with *Joseph in Ägypten.*

In the same year, 1926, the Social Democratic government of the
state of Prussia established a Sektion für Dichtkunst (Section for
Literary Art) in the Academy of Arts in Berlin. The intent was to
draw Germany's literary authors closer to the republic. Thomas
supported the move; he was one of the founding members with
Heinrich by his side. The effort yielded only partial success: some
writers chose to stay away; nationalistic writers attempted to use
the academy to further their anti-democratic goals.

Thomas Mann had been reading Sigmund Freud's publications
since 1925; *Totem and Taboo* (1913) became his favoured work while
he developed the Joseph theme. When the 'Club of Democratic
Students' of the University of Munich asked him to give a lecture, he
offered 'Die Stellung Freuds in der modernen Geistesgeschichte' (1929;
Freud's Position in the History of Modern Thought). He praises *Totem
and Taboo* as reflecting *Humanität*, and Freud's psychoanalysis as
both succeeding the Romantic protest against rational materialism
and a new Enlightenment resisting reactionary abuse.

With Katia Mann's parents, Alfred and Hedwig Pringsheim, in Nidden, 1930.

By 1927 Mann came more and more into conflict with the nationalist bourgeois press. A journalist, after discovering deletions in a new edition of *Betrachtungen eines Unpolitischen*, accused the author of falsifying its nationalistic intent. Mann assured his public that he had omitted only hostile polemics.

The novella 'Mario und der Zauberer' (1930; Mario and the Magician), written in 1929, is based on Mann's direct experience with Italian fascism three years earlier, when Mussolini had become dictator. During a family summer holiday at the Italian coast, Mann had experienced the misuse of power under the cover of national pride. In his story, Cipolla, a magician presenting himself as a fascist nobleman, forces the audience to submit to his will. He succeeds in bridging the space between himself and his public in a malicious way by humiliating the test people he selects. Cipolla's performance becomes an exaggerated and negative image of the power the writer wants to gain over his readers. 'Freedom exists,' Cipolla says, 'and also the will exists, but freedom of the will does not exist' (*GW* VIII, 689; *SL* II, 195). Mann has him think in terms of Schopenhauer's philosophy that gives freedom only to the impersonal 'Will'.

Cipolla is able to bend the 'Will' in his direction; it is the fluid that surges between the magician and his audience, with Cipolla in command. He humiliates those who resist him. Yet his nearly flawless performance is the admirable achievement of an outsider.

Since Mann's children called their father *Zauberer* (magician), is he indicting himself as a writer who might misuse his power over an audience? Did he design Cipolla as an ambivalent figure in order to avoid being judged guilty of bias? In 1929 and 1930 biased right-wing literature abounded in Germany. Perhaps Mann wanted to set a positive example with 'Mario und der Zauberer'. He lets the story end violently: Mario avenges himself after Cipolla, convinced that he does not need to respect the waiter, lures him into a kiss meant for his beloved. Although the figure of Mario appears only on the last pages, the novella carries the title 'Mario and the Magician'. Murdering Cipolla is the liberating act that outweighs all the magician's remarkable skills. It was wishful thinking in 1929.[1]

In November of that year the Swedish Academy awarded Thomas Mann the Nobel Prize in Literature. He received much public recognition on that occasion, but the nationalist, and

The Nobel Prize in Literature, 1929.

especially the National Socialist, press became ever more hostile towards him over his support of the republic. As the Western world began to suffer under the Great Depression following the stock market crash in the United States in October 1929, unemployment grew rapidly. German elections in September 1930 reflected a general disaffection: Adolf Hitler's Nazi Party increased its seats in the Reichstag from twelve to 107. The Communists won seats as well. Attempts by the Reichspräsident to govern authoritatively with emergency decrees brought no relief; the disaffection increased.

Startled by the increasing voting power of the National Socialists, Mann decided to address his readers, the *Bildungsbürger*, with 'Deutsche Ansprache: Ein Appell an die Vernunft' (1930; An Appeal to Reason). After initially agreeing with his audience about the necessity of protesting the Versailles Treaty, he turns with disdain to the National Socialist Party, branding its ideology as false Romanticism and false Modernism. The party that promoted the national community and its real interests was the Social Democratic Party, he insisted. But few burghers followed his advice. When, in 1931, he addressed students at his former Gymnasium in Lübeck, arguing against the call for a leader (*Führer*), he was hissed and his voice silenced by insistent shuffling of feet ('Ansprache an die Jugend'; 1931; *GW* x, 316–27). He had better luck talking to Social Democrats in Vienna.

The year 1932 was the centenary of Goethe's death. Mann had prepared extensively for a book on Goethe. Whatever he had in mind did not materialize, but he used his studies for two lectures. One placed Goethe in the history of the bourgeois age, what we would call 'modernity', beginning in the eighteenth century or even in the Renaissance; the other celebrated Goethe as the writer (*Schriftsteller*) of the nation.

While Mann publicly held firm to the illusion that the majority of Germans would not tolerate a Nazi takeover, his private letters reflect fear of a totalitarian and chauvinistic regime. On 30 January

Lecture tour for the Goethe Jubilee, Berlin, 1932.

1933, when Reichspräsident Hindenburg appointed Hitler as the chancellor of a coalition government, and the new government was confirmed by a majority vote in the Reichstag, he still thought he was safe in Bavaria, where clerical parties held the majority.

On the invitation of Munich's Goethe Society, Mann presented the lecture 'Leiden und Grösse Richard Wagners' (1933; Sufferings and Greatness of Richard Wagner) on 10 February 1933. The audience applauded. When Mann and his wife left for Amsterdam, Brussels and Paris on the following day with plans to repeat the Wagner lecture there (in Brussels and Paris in French), both were unaware that they would not return home. They had planned on a winter holiday, but they soon heard of the arbitrary persecution of regime critics, especially in Munich where the police had quickly come under the control of the Nazis. We know now that the police had orders to arrest Thomas Mann at the border, ready to intern him in a concentration camp.

The couple's residence in Munich was soon impounded; a few personal items, including Mann's desk and part of his library, were transported to friends in Switzerland, among them the manuscript, notes and source books for the four-part novel *Joseph und seine Brüder* (1943; *Joseph and his Brothers*).[2] Thomas had started his research on the novel in 1925 during the relatively good years of the Weimar Republic. The biblical story provided him with an opportunity for fictionalizing a vision: a narcissistic but intelligent and creative outsider would adapt to the world and become a beneficial leader of people.

In March of that year Mann had briefly visited temples in Egypt during a Mediterranean cruise. A second journey with his wife in February 1930 had led both to Upper Egypt and to the Museum of Cairo. They were guided by Wilhelm Spiegelberg, Professor of Egyptology at the University of Munich, who continued to be at hand with information. From Cairo the Manns travelled to Jerusalem and Palestine.

Among the study material for the Joseph project was a book that traced the Jewish Bible to its oriental background: Alfred Jeremias's *The Old Testament in the Light of the Ancient East* (1911).[3] Jeremias shows how biblical motifs have their precursors in oriental myths. Mann's special library on the Arabian Orient and Egypt steadily increased and is largely preserved.

Throughout *Joseph und seine Brüder* the narrator establishes a humorous relationship with the reader by asserting that he did not invent his stories; he had rather relied on the 'facts of tradition' (*Tatsachen der Überlieferung*), which he calls unshakeable (FA VII.1, 244; *JW*, 226). But these 'facts' are often shaken. An example is Mann's linking of Jacob's dream about the heavenly ladder with his defeat by Esau's son Eliphas. The latter episode does not appear in the biblical account; Mann added it from non-biblical Hebrew sources. Many details refer to the myths of gods other than Abraham's God and move these myths into a much closer relationship to Abraham's tribe than the Bible will allow.

The Manns visiting Upper Egypt, 1930.

Mann began to write 'Vorspiel: Höllenfahrt' (Prelude: Descent into Hell) at the end of 1926. The narrator accompanies the reader while descending into 'mankind's past', a time when Abraham had been migrating from the Babylonian kingdom, making contact with his supreme deity in the desert along the way. Mann's narration lets the biblical events play in a mythical world, where the self is determined by the patterns of forebears and time is understood as circular rather than linear and fixed. In *Der junge Joseph* (1934; *Young Joseph*), the second novel, Eliezer, Jacob's mentor, identifies himself with the mentor of Abraham, who is not Jacob's actual grandfather but has lived long ago.

Chapters at the end of the prelude combine gnostic speculations about matter, soul and spirit (or intelligence; in German *Geist*) with stories about angels and the Fall of Lucifer. The source for this playful piece is a collection of Jewish tales by Micha Josef Bin Gorion.[4] Mann expands the biblical text, using Jewish and Islamic legends. At the end of this prelude, the author anticipates Jacob's final blessings for Joseph: from heaven as well as from Earth, from spirit as well as from matter. The narrator, speaking for the author, invokes the same blessings for the book.

The reader meets Joseph in the first chapter of *Die Geschichten Jaakobs* (1933; *The Stories of Jacob*), sitting at a well outside his father's camp near Hebron in what is now Palestine. He is singing to the moon and stars when his anxious father, Jacob (spelled Jaakob), is looking for him. Jacob had founded his family and had raised a large herd of sheep while living with his relative Laban; about his life there we will hear later on.

Joseph has a lively interest in the myths of other gods, although he adheres loyally to the god of his fathers. But despite worshipping a supreme deity, Jacob's and Joseph's world is still a world of myths, understood as a rolling sphere. A heavenly and an earthly hemisphere are corresponding with one another (*FA* VII.I, 145; *JW*, 151). 'Stories come down from above, just as a god becomes man;

they . . . become earthly, but do not cease to play up above and be narratable in that form' (*FA* VII.I, 413; cf. *JW*, 353).[5]

Jacob's life is not a model for a recognizable morality. Questionable events begin with him stealing the blessing from his brother Esau, which the narrator justifies because Esau is less suitable for developing the image of God than his brother. God does not react when Jacob's sons assault Sichem, while using circumcision, the symbol of the covenant, to deceive the Sichemites. Thomas Mann's Abraham had found out: 'He [God] is not the good. He is the Whole' (*FA* VII.I, 406; cf. *JW*, 348). The god of Abraham and Jacob does not guarantee universal ethics.

Jacob's flight to Laban in Mesopotamia begins a narration in chronological order, foregrounding the events surrounding Jacob's family in a quasi-realistic fashion, with the mythical world active in the background. God's design moves the events. Minor gods exist, blessings create fortunes, miracles occur, and Jacob increases his flock of sheep in an unscientific way. These are accepted features within the fictional reality of a world in the fourteenth century BCE.

In the sub-chapter 'Von Gottes Eifersucht' (God's Jealousy), the narrator entertains the reasons for Leah's abundant fertility, while Rachel (Mann says Rahel) remains barren for many years: God is jealous of Jacob's preponderance of feelings and needs to restrain it. The same God defends his prerogative to diffuse his grace to whomever he chooses. Jacob's God has some qualities of the passionate desert god Yahoo in him. God is still in the process of developing. This is modern theology, not the biblical one.

An aside in the novel may reveal something of Thomas Mann's own beliefs. Following Rachel's death, God remains silent to Jacob's plea: 'Lord what are you doing?' The narrator continues with his own thoughts: 'In such cases, there is no answer. Yet it is the glory of human souls that the silence does not make them turn away from God but enables them to grasp the majesty of what is incomprehensible, using it to grow' (*FA* VII.I, 358; cf. *JW*, 313). Real greatness is incalculable.

Die Geschichten Jaakobs was published in 1933 by Samuel Fischer in Berlin, the year Adolf Hitler seized power. The Jewish firm continued to operate in Berlin until 1936; Thomas Mann was in exile in Switzerland.

The second part, *Der junge Joseph*, vivifies the story of Genesis, Chapter 37. Thomas augments the biblical account by detailing Joseph's education. Joseph learns from Jacob's steward Eliezer how Abraham discovered God. Insisting on serving only the highest being, Abraham finds God in the traditional way, using the ontological proof of God's existence: since God is the greatest, his existence cannot be negated. God is both outside of Abraham – he expresses happiness for being discovered (*FA* VII.I, 400; *JW*, 344) – and also within him, since Abraham has 'thought Him into being' (*hervorgedacht*) (*FA* VII.I, 402; *JW*, 346). Since God is the Whole, he is both good and evil (*FA* VII.I, 405; *JW*, 347). Again, this is Thomas Mann's theology. But the sub-chapter, 'How Abraham Discovers God', is not ironic; its reverence for the idea of something exalted and holy is genuine.

Abraham's God is not yet universal. Other deities exist in the world of 1300 BCE, and the sub-chapter 'Der Adonishain' (The Grove of Adonai) suggests Joseph's attachment to the shepherd god Tammuz Adonai. Joseph takes his brother Benjamin to a grove consecrated to this god. Lovingly, he shares the secret with his younger brother, the one who is not envious and hostile like the older brothers from Leah. Joseph explains to Benjamin how the women re-enact the divine myth: a young god lies dead in the grove with a wound in his side. Describing the mourning women, Mann uses a line from the Passion of St Matthew by Johann Sebastian Bach (*FA* VII.I, 427: 'Wir setzen uns mit Tränen nieder'; cf. *JW*, 364: 'we sit down amidst tears'). The author activates his readers' Christian religious feelings. Joseph wears a myrtle wreath as a sign of self-sacrifice, and Adonai, the Lord, rises from his grave. A young woman announces his resurrection.

Joseph's role as Jacob's favourite, his intellectual superiority and his narcissistic dreams make him an outsider among his brothers, and he uses his father's excessive love to obtain the 'coat of many colours'. The novel identifies the coat with the bridal veil of Rachel, the 'Ketônet'. It is embroidered with representations of mythical scenes and figures, most of all of Ishtar, the goddess of sex and fertility (*FA* VII.I, 257, 259–61; *JW*, 236, 238). Wearing the veil, Joseph arrogates the power of Ishtar to himself, assuming a female dimension. 'I and the mother are one,' he says to Ruben (*FA* VII.I, 481; cf. *JW*, 405).

While his brothers beat him, Joseph loses his certainty that all people must love him more than themselves. But Mann's story solicits tolerance for the brothers. When they haul Joseph, naked and bound, to the dry well, they can feel the tenderness of his skin (*FA* VII.I, 553; *JW*, 460). These are homoerotic feelings, suggested by what follows: 'What they had done onto their brother, they had done out of jealousy.' Jealousy, a distorted form of love (*FA* VII.I, 554; cf. *JW*, 461); the beating was a perversion of homoerotic love.

The man in the field is an angel who knows what Joseph's destiny will be, but he is not allowed to let him know that he partakes of God's omniscience. The scene is a humorous play with the theological concept.

In order to become able to understand his destiny, Joseph must first break through his narcissism. He does so in the pit, acknowledging his fate of having to become an outsider in Egypt who must learn to adjust to his social environment. Only then can he become a saviour of Egyptians and of his family, the family who will, in turn, produce another saviour. When the stone is moved from the dry well, Joseph rises as if from his grave, a scene alluding to the resurrection of Jesus. The seventh and final chapter of *Der junge Joseph*, narrating Jacob's mourning, is inspired by the Book of Job, the tale of the incalculability of God's grace. *Der junge Joseph* was also published in Berlin in 1934.

Thomas Mann in Sanary-sur-Mer, France, 1933.

6

Joseph and his Author in Exile, *Lotte in Weimar*

On 19 February 1933, the Manns were in Paris where Thomas had delivered the French version of his Wagner lecture. On the same day in Berlin, a message he had written in support of the republic and a humane form of socialism was read aloud in a social democratic cultural meeting. It received wide and often unfavourable notice in the press, and Mann quickly decided to abandon his public role in his home country. A more intimate blow followed: a written protest against the content of his Wagner lecture, published on 16 April 1933 in *Münchener Neueste Nachrichten*, the middle-class paper that had turned hostile towards him. Forty-two professors, artists and officials, with only a few National Socialists among them, had signed the document, accusing Mann of belittling Wagner, a great national mind. He was not surprised by the hostilities of the Nazis, but most of the signers were *Bildungsbürger*. He began a new diary in Arosa, relating his 'morbid horror' that the foundation of his life had suddenly changed.

During the summer of 1933, Thomas, Katia and the youngest children moved to the French Riviera, where they joined other exiled German writers, among them brother Heinrich. Mann's older children, Klaus, Erika and Golo, urged him to declare his opposition to the regime, but he refrained from any direct public attack for three years. His silence was the condition under which his books could still appear in Germany. The first two Joseph volumes, published in 1933 and 1934, sold well. But there was a cost for his silence.

Mann's son Klaus had started a literary journal, *Die Sammlung* (The Collection), in the Netherlands. It was open to German writers no longer allowed to publish in their homeland. The first edition listed the names of authors who had agreed to publish in the journal, among them Thomas Mann. A political article by Klaus's uncle Heinrich in that issue caught the attention of a new supervisory authority in control of Germany's book trade; it directed all bookshops to boycott contributors to the journal. The Fischer publishing house negotiated an agreement with the agency, cancelling the boycott under the condition that all writers wishing to continue publishing in Germany withdraw from *Die Sammlung*. Thomas reluctantly agreed. The incident disturbed the relationship with his older children, Klaus and Erika, who wanted their father to sever his relationship with Fischer and publish with an exile publisher.

In September 1933 the Manns and the younger children moved into a rented house in Küsnacht near Zurich, where they lived until their move to the United States in 1938. In June 1934 Alfred Knopf, Thomas's American publisher in New York, organized festivities for a joint celebration of Mann's 59th birthday and the English-language publication of *Young Joseph*; the journey established contacts for the Manns in the United States.

During the summer of 1934, he interrupted *Joseph in Ägypten*, starting work on a political essay about the damage to German culture inflicted by National Socialism. But he abandoned the article and wrote a narrative work instead: 'Meerfahrt mit Don Quijote' (1935; Voyage with Don Quixote), a fictional diary inspired by his reading of Miguel de Cervantes's *Don Quixote*. The work would not create difficulties for the Fischer publishing firm – still holding out in Berlin – or Swiss neutrality. Cervantes, a believing Christian and the king's loyal subject, writes about Spanish Muslims forced to emigrate; the king had declared their conversion to Christianity untrustworthy. Mann echoes Cervantes's account of their suffering:

Spain had not become purer but poorer through the extirpation (*Ausmerzung*) of the Muslims. 'Meerfahrt mit Don Quijote' became part of a volume of essays, *Leiden und Grösse der Meister*, which appeared in Berlin in 1935. During a second American journey, 11 June to 12 July 1935, Thomas received a honorary doctorate from Harvard University and was invited to a White House dinner, meeting President Franklin D. Roosevelt and his wife, Eleanor.

Erika and Klaus Mann had been deprived of their German citizenship in 1935, but the Nazi authorities hesitated to do the same to their father. The German Nobel Prize winner was too well known. When Eduard Korrodi, feuilleton editor of *Neue Zürcher Zeitung*, made a distinction between him and the activity of German exiles in Paris who published a German language weekly opposing the Nazi regime, Mann reacted with a letter to Korrodi, published in the Zurich paper *Das Neue Tagebuch* in February 1936, in which he declared his solidarity with the German exiles, daring the regime to denaturalize him. He avoids the country, he writes, where he has deeper roots than those who 'waver for three years whether they will deny me my Germanness for all the world to see'. He accuses the Nazis of abandoning the roots of European culture, Christianity and classical antiquity, their anti-Semitism taking aim at those very roots (*EK* IV, 169–74). In May of the same year, Thomas and Katia travelled to Vienna, where Mann delivered his lecture 'Freud und die Zukunft' (Freud and the Future) celebrating Freud's eightieth birthday. He called Freud a pioneer in the propagation of the new humanism, the religious concern for human rights and welfare he himself had been advocating.

On 5 December 1936, with the Olympic Games completed, the German government lifted Thomas Mann's citizenship together with that of his wife and children Golo, Elisabeth and Michael. But this action had no effect; a Czech citizen had already arranged in November for the naturalization of the Manns in a small Czechoslovakian community. Soon afterwards, the University of Bonn revoked the honorary philosophical doctorate Mann had received in 1919. The Swiss publisher Oprecht printed the University Dean's short notice, together with Mann's reply, in a brochure in January 1937 under the title 'Ein Briefwechsel' (An Exchange of Letters). Mann's response cited the rationale already given for his recent honorary doctorate from Harvard University: he had preserved the dignity of Germany's culture. Mann used the opportunity to expose the 'incomparable moral significance' of the events happening in Germany. The present regime threatens the world with its arms production designed for war, he declares, a war that can no longer be permitted in Europe. A prayer ends the 'Exchange': 'May God help the misused country and let it make peace with the world and itself' (*EK* IV, 183–91).

Mann returned to the third part of the Joseph novel, *Joseph in Ägypten* (1936; Joseph in Egypt), in May 1933. Throughout the beginning of the volume, Joseph interprets his being taken to Egypt as the will of God, blocking all thoughts of escaping the desert merchant to whom his brothers had sold him. His destiny is now focused on a goal: he will become provider and saviour. Time is no longer circular for Joseph, although the mythical world around him has not changed.

Joseph's preliminary rise in status, from slave to man of importance in the house of Potiphar, or Peteprê, as Thomas names him, succeeds in the manner of a fairy tale. Flat characters flank the hero: the two dwarfs, the devoted Gottlieb and the dishonest Dûdu. But the fairy-tale approach does not dominate the work. Inner complexity is given to Mut-em-enet and to Peteprê: Mut-em-enet expands her role as a token wife, while Peteprê rebels against his emasculation, although not overtly; the reader concludes it from his actions. The narrator, although frequently informing the reader of the characters' thoughts, gives Peteprê the role of an outsider who, like his author, does not want to share his encumbrance.

During Joseph's purchase in Peteprê's house, the narrator cautiously suggests divine action. Peteprê's overseer, while initially unwilling to purchase him, is moved to do so when looking into Joseph's eyes. The narrator adds: 'It is possible – we are merely offering a supposition, not venturing an assertion – that at this very moment, on which so much depended, the planning God of Joseph's fathers went out of his way for Joseph and let fall upon him a ray of light, capable of producing the intended effect in the heart of the gazing man.' The narrator is willing to withdraw his suggestion if the supernatural quality of this 'natural story' should appear to be inappropriate (*FA* VIII.I, 819; cf. *JW*, 650). Close to his author here, the narrator speaks to the modern reader and is uncertain whether he should speak of a living God in a way that might be read as transcending fiction.

The question of whether a living God can count as a fictional character in a novel surfaces again when Mont-kaw, the overseer who has befriended Joseph, dies. His illness and death are narrated in lovingly painful detail, as they would be in a naturalistic novel. Yet God, guiding Joseph's destiny, wills Mont-kaw's death so that Joseph may rise. Joseph still feels guilt; everything originates with God, he concludes, but we become guilty before him. 'Man bears God's guilt and it would be only fair, if someday God would decide to bear our guilt' (*FA* VIII.I, 102; cf. *JW*, 803). The allusion to Christian doctrine is humorous but not without serious connotations. The theology of the unreliable narrator of *Joseph und seine Brüder* is incalculable. Once, when Joseph discusses God with the Pharaoh in *Joseph der Ernährer* (1943; *Joseph the Provider*), he gives God the qualities of Schopenhauer's 'Will': 'He has neither space nor time, and though the world is in Him, yet He is not in the world but in heaven,' which is out of this world (*FA* VIII.I, 1539; cf. *JW*, 1196).

When Joseph learns that Peteprê was emasculated as a child, elements of Johann Jakob Bachofen's theories of the sequence of cultural eras come into play. Bachofen, in the mid-nineteenth century, posited an original polyamorous hetaerism as a primitive social order without laws, followed, still in prehistory, by matriarchy, a social organization with some laws and politically dominated by women. Bachofen replaced this culture with a monarchic, patriarchic one with stricter laws and sexual rules, extending to historic times. When Joseph serves Peteprê's parents, Huij and Tuij (Woods translates them as 'Huya and Tuya'), he learns how they had lived in an Egyptian sibling marriage, described in Bachofen's terms as polyamorous. Expecting the coming of a new religion of light with severe sexual rules, they decide to sacrifice to the new age by castrating their son. But they suffer from guilt and fear punishment by the judge of the dead (*FA* VIII.1, 889–903; *JW*, 703–14). Their fear, and Joseph's condemnation of what the parents did, turn the reader against the Romantic application of Bachofen; the sacrifice for a new order results in an unhappy son. While Peteprê's condition enables him to rise to a high position at court, it has destined him to an outsider status and destroys his self-worth.

Joseph, while still a slave, wins the trust and affection of his owner, the emasculated Peteprê, by a speech about the relativity of sexual differences. A long chapter records the futile love of Mut-em-enet, Peteprê's wife, taking up the theme of Mann's 'Die Geliebten': a hopeless love from a woman's perspective. Mann himself had experienced another futile love in 1927: a homoerotic attraction to a young man from Düsseldorf, Klaus Heuser, on the island of Sylt in the North Sea. The encounter was more gratifying than the Paul Ehrenberg affair; Heuser, himself bisexual, was congenial, but this encounter was frustrated as well. Heuser was eighteen in 1927, and Thomas could not win the young man's interest in his writing. An embrace and a kiss were the only physical expressions of desire Thomas allowed himself.[1]

The narrator, taking up the position of the author, calls a force, breaking into a seemingly well-constructed existence

Klaus Heuser and Elisabeth Mann, *c*. 1928.

as Mut-em-enet's, a 'visitation' (*FA* VIII.I, 1123; *JW*, 881–2).
It is similar to what Herr Friedeman or Aschenbach in 'Der
Tod in Venedig' had experienced. All three 'visitations' are
fictional transformations of Mann's own experiences, as can
be shown by Mut-em-enet's prayer of thank you for being enriched
by her love. Mann used a poem he had recorded in his notebook
during his infatuation with Paul Ehrenberg (*FA* VIII.I, 1153–5;
NB II, 44, 46).

Joseph is affected by Mut-em-enet's love, but he must not deviate
from his divinely mandated destiny. He tries to shift her passion into
useful activity by engaging her in discussions about the household
economy. When, after years of futile longing, Mut finally reaches
out for him, Joseph is sexually aroused, yet he still persuades her to
relinquish her desire. The text describes this event as a conflict of
spirit (*Geist*) and body in Joseph (*FA* VIII.I, 1312; *JW*, 1024), evoking
the dualism of Plato, St Paul, Kant and Schopenhauer that coexists
in Thomas Mann's world view with the monistic tendency of God
understood as the Whole. The seven reasons the text offers for
Joseph's 'chastity'– his willingness to resist Mut's desire – refer more
to his loyalty to God, his father, to Mont-kaw and to Potiphar than
constituting a catalogue of sexual sins. One of the reasons for
Joseph's resistance lies in Mut's assuming the role of a suitor,
denying him an elevated male role (*FA* VIII.I, 1181; *JW*, 925). Author
and narrator seem to agree on male superiority, betraying how
much the modernist Thomas Mann is still influenced by his
nineteenth-century upbringing.

Mut-em-enet's speech to Potiphar's people parodies the racist
propaganda of the Nazis. With it the narrator abandons his
sympathetic depiction of Mut. Potiphar's judgement is a surprise;
it departs from the biblical narrative that recounts Potiphar's
'anger' or 'wrath'. Mann's Potiphar judges with prudent composure;
he is an outsider, a careful observer from a distance, enabling him to
deliver a just verdict. *Joseph in Egypt*, completed on 23 August 1936,

was published in October 1937 in Vienna, the Fischer publishing firm's new location.

Among ideas for future projects, always occupying Mann, was a plan to put Goethe on his narrative stage. In 1911, at the time of 'Der Tod in Venedig', he had temporarily considered taking up the story of Goethe's embarrassment over unfulfilled marriage plans in Marienbad. In 1931, while preparing for the centennial of Goethe's death, Mann discovered a surprising discussion of the poet's love life by Felix Theilhaber: instead of living out his love affairs, Goethe had transformed his experiences into poetry.[2] In 1936, the theme, so close to Mann's own practice, not only offered a welcome change from the biblical topic, having by now occupied him for more than ten years, but provided the opportunity to let Goethe comment on Germany. Theilhaber's book became one of the most important sources for Mann's image of Goethe; his copy with pencil markings and marginal notes is preserved in the Thomas-Mann-Archive in Zurich.[3] While admiring Goethe, Theilhaber opposed the near-religious veneration of his life and work widespread among Germans in 1932.

In March 1935, Mann re-read the story of Charlotte Kestner's visit in Weimar in 1816 in Theilhaber's book (Diary, 23 March 1935). In 1772, Goethe had met Charlotte, who became Lotte Buff in his novel *The Sorrows of Young Werther* (1774). Theilhaber quoted from a novelist who called himself Belani and who had narrated episodes from Goethe's love life, embellished with anecdotal inventions.[4] In his story of Charlotte's visit of 1816, Belani asserts that she had appeared in Goethe's house in a white dress with red ribbons resembling the one she had worn 1772 in Wetzlar. When Goethe missed the allusion, Belani writes, Charlotte was offended. Theilhaber seems to have believed Belani's anecdote of Charlotte's dress to be true. It was most likely Belani's invention, but it made a good story for Thomas Mann.

In November 1936 he started writing what he first intended to be a novella under the title 'Wiedersehen' (Reunion).[5] The story opens with a scene joining humour and sincerity typical of Mann's style. Mager, a waiter working for the Hotel Zum Elefanten in Weimar, 'a cultured person' (*ein gebildeter Mann*; *FA* IX.I, 11; cf. *LL*, 3), learns that the elderly woman who had just arrived was the Lotte of Goethe's *Werther*. Having read the novel five times, he is overjoyed to see her, using the opportunity to ask, quoting from *Werther*, if the farewell scene at the end of the first book, 'We will see each other again, we will find each other, among all shapes [*Gestalten*], we will recognize each other' (*FA* IX.I, 24–5; cf. *LL*, 18), had really happened.[6] Mager wants to know whether Goethe believes in a reunion after death, perhaps to overcome his own doubt.

The belief in a reunion, being able to meet and recognize loved ones in an afterworld, was long seen as a promise of the Christian faith. The disappearance of metaphysical certainty is a theme in all of Mann's works. Belief in recognizing loved ones after death is treated ironically at the end of *Buddenbrooks* but contrasted by the senator's finding a substitute religion in Schopenhauer's essay on death. Mager's question shows him guided by the popular confusion between fiction and its template in real life. The author has Lotte evade the answer: she says, 'yes and no' (*FA* IX.I, 25; *LL*, 8). Fiction relates to the reality of author and reader but has transmuted and changed it.

Mager introduces a series of characters visiting Charlotte in the inn and offering perspectives on Goethe. To Friedrich Wilhelm Riemer, Goethe's former assistant, Charlotte confesses what had made her travel to Weimar: the desire to settle an old score (*FA* IX.I, 106; *LL*, 99). In 1772 in Wetzlar, Goethe had pursued her, she complained, had aroused her feelings and encouraged them, had estranged her from her fiancé. Then Goethe had suddenly left and written his novel, merely sending a few letters. In a moment of anger, she calls this conduct towards an engaged woman parasitic, no more than 'Schmarutzertum' (*FA* IX.I, 117; *LL*, 110). Freeloader or parasite (*Schmarotzer*) is the word that Heinrich Mann had hurled at his brother Thomas in his biographical essay 'Zola' of 1915, meaning a writer who is not socially engaged.

Riemer justifies the writer's autonomy to Charlotte in religious terms, and according to Mann the writer enjoys a God-like position vis-à-vis the world, he insists. God, being the Whole, the entirety, is not ruled by perspectives and controlled by individual purposes like human beings or even the writer's characters. Poetry is free of responsibility. Riemer had characterized Goethe earlier as an all-embracing great being, but also as cold and nihilistic (*FA* IX.I, 88–90; *LL*, 82–3), similar to Joseph with his double blessing of spirit and nature. Because Riemer has sacrificed much of his life in the service of Goethe, he understands Lotte well, but living near greatness and speaking its language have not prevented him from becoming a subaltern character.

Adele Schopenhauer, the philosopher's sister and another caller, has known Goethe from his visits to her mother's salon. Her Goethe is the private, intimate person who can be ordinary, even inconsiderate, since nobody dares to attack the great man. The purpose of Adele calling on Lotte is to solicit her help in preventing the marriage of her friend Ottilie von Pogwisch to Goethe's son August, whose uneven character she finds wanting. Her long story involves Christiane, Goethe's sweetheart and later wife, who was slighted by Weimar society, especially after their marriage in 1806. Weimar society extends the contempt to her son August, after his father, using his privileges, disallows his son's plan of 1813 to join the war against Napoleon. Goethe, fond of the youthful Ottilie, seeks to persuade her to marry August despite her misgivings. It is a selfish move that reduces his stature.

Adele's circle is friendly to Prussia, supporting the war of liberation, while Goethe sympathizes with Napoleon and his reorganization of the Continent. But since Adele admires Goethe, she provides his perspective in spite of her own opposition. The alliances forming against Napoleon in 1813, however, change sympathies in Weimar: Adele observes that such developing political fronts can give licence to social snubs, as they were aimed at Goethe's son August (*FA* IX.I, 202; *LL*, 179).

The next visitor is August himself carrying the dinner invitation for Lotte to his father's house. After complaining about Weimar society's disdain for his mother, he talks about his father's frequent infirmities, his 'endangered friendship with life' (*FA* IX.I, 233; cf. *LL*, 229). Goethe has recently abandoned plans for a journey to the Frankfurt area where he planned to meet the new muse of his *West-Eastern Divan*, Marianne, the foster child of his friend Johann Jacob Willemer. Although Goethe's poems speak of his love for Marianne, and although she had answered in Goethe's lyrical style, after his friend Willemer has married Marianne, the lover Goethe feels eased rather than hampered: his love poems are now aimed at the wife of a friend and less at a personal lover. He is giving lasting value to the relationship in the poems of *West-Eastern Divan* while forsaking the living Marianne, much as he had Friederike Brion, Goethe's first muse, whose fate August had just movingly described, and, of course, Lotte herself. The destinies of all three women fit into Theilhaber's explanation of Goethe's love lyrics as the sublimation of an abnormal sexuality.

The seventh chapter presents Goethe himself in a stream-of-consciousness monologue. Most detail can be verified, but elements are fused, producing Thomas Mann's own Goethe, whom he has waking up erotically excited by a dream of an Italian painting of Venus. The 67-year-old man is proud of his potency, but his youthful exuberance has limits: he has gout in his arm. The stream of consciousness yields contradictions: Goethe misses Friedrich Schiller, who had died eleven years earlier. He had been happy with Schiller's stimulation and encouragements, his understanding of *Faust*, but he also asks himself: 'Did I ever like him?' The answer is: 'Never' (*FA* IX.I, 287; *LL*, 286). While productive thoughts in Mann's

Goethe revolve around the Helena scene and the classical Walpurgis Night of *Faust*, he mentions the tragedy of Gretchen in passing, as Faust's 'pitifully narrow story with the girl' (*FA* IX.I, 349; cf. *LL*, 353).

The scene with the scribe, John, contrasts Goethe's free poetic imagination with the Weimar official supporting law and order. The scribe wants a recommendation for a position in the Prussian censor's office. Mann's Goethe promises the letter, while despising John's submissiveness. Goethe likes his servant Carl better but dismisses him once he contracts syphilis. His imagination diverts to the idea for a story set in a bordello where love degenerates into cruelty, but the event cannot be brought to life, considering society as it is. 'Alas, what strong and extraordinary subjects I could offer if I lived in a free and ingenious society!' he laments (*FA* IX.I, 303; cf. *LL*, 303). But the same Goethe opposes the freedom of the press: censorship and taboos are challenges beneficial to good journalists.

Thomas Mann shapes his Goethe similar to himself: Goethe has a darker-skinned grandmother who lived near the Roman frontier and thus might be a descendant of the inhabitants of the Roman province Germania, as Mann often mentions his Portuguese grandmother. He lets Goethe understand the homoerotic perspective of Johann Joachim Winckelmann when looking at classical statues, remembering having seen beauty himself, often in the young female form, 'but not absolutely'. He shows him admiring the serenity in a young, fair-haired waiter who served as a model for poems in the 'Book of the Tavern and the Tavern-boy' in *West-Eastern Divan* (*FA* IX.I; 352–3; *LL*, 357).[7]

An outline for the poem 'Paria' (Pariah) about seduction in an Indian setting now arises in Goethe's imagination. Seduction had been Goethe's playbook for Lotte in 1772, having produced *Werther*. Now Marianne von Willemer is the object of the new playbook *West-Eastern Divan*. One of the poems uses a metaphor to describe the unique power a poet employs when he turns reality into poetic form: if the poet dips his pure hands into water, water will fuse into a ball (*FA* IX.I, 356; *LL*, 360).[8]

Mann wanted to expose the stiff older Goethe, he changed the dinner's setting from a familial gathering to a larger affair and had him appear in formal attire 'with a silver star, a Weimar order of merit on his chest' (*FA* IX.I, 386; *LL*, 392). The chapter is narrated from Charlotte's point of view. She notices how Goethe is repulsed by her presence despite his polite conversation, and she observes his attention to the involuntary nodding of her head. She does not find an opportunity to utter her accusation and drops the idea altogether. Goethe's monologue dominates the conversation with the guests eagerly listening. When he cites an alleged Chinese proverb, 'A great man is a public catastrophe' (*FA* IX.I, 411; cf. *LL*, 418), all his guests erupt into laughter except Charlotte; the obedient mirth disturbs her. Thomas has his Goethe mention a medieval pogrom in the town of Eger: like Jews, he opines, Germans are hated. He fears a global consensus; it is Mann's message to the German people of 1939.

Lotte in Weimar concludes with a late-night meeting between Lotte and her former beloved in his coach, lent to her for a visit to the theatre. When she enters the carriage for the ride back to her hotel, she finds Goethe sitting in the rear corner. It is a different Goethe, existing perhaps merely in Lotte's imagination, despite relating to the events at the earlier dinner. This Goethe understands her reproach in having worn the special dress and apologizes, and she withdraws her complaint. Goethe's poems and the novel *The Sufferings of Young Werther* have transformed a fleeting love encounter into lasting poetry. Goethe explains the transformation, paraphrasing his poem 'Selige Sehnsucht' (Blessed Longing) from *West-Eastern Divan*: the poet offers a sacrifice, being both celebrant and sacrificial victim, both candle and flame. Burning, he consumes himself while attracting the moth that flies into the candle, becoming one with it in death.[9]

7

In America: The Second World War and *Joseph the Provider*

The start of 1937 found Thomas Mann in good spirits. The letter to the University of Bonn, 'Ein Briefwechsel', with its strong warning against the Nazi regime as a danger to peace, saw several printings and appeared translated in London. A Swiss socialist women's association asked for an appendix to its book on the Spanish Civil War. The English translation carried the title 'I Stand with the Spanish People' (*EK* IV, 192–7).[1] Mann's support for Spain's socialist government was a minority opinion in the Western world. The *Neue Zürcher Zeitung*, for example, distrusted Spanish socialists because of their association with the small Communist Party. As a guest in Switzerland, Mann had to employ caution when speaking out against Nazi Germany, but a new cultural bimonthly, *Mass und Wert* (Measure and Value), funded by a wealthy Luxembourgian woman, gave him a voice. He served as principal, though not managing, editor. The first issue, September/October 1937, contained a programmatic essay by the editor and the first chapter of Mann's *Lotte in Weimar*. Lack of quality submissions led to the journal's closure in 1940. It was difficult to find articles that managed to remain above the political struggle between Marxism and fascism.

A third trip to the United States, in April 1937, served to support the University in Exile in New York, a part of the New School for Social Research open to scholars who had been dismissed in fascist countries. During the short visit, Mann hardly noticed an event that turned out to be most important for his future: he was interviewed by Agnes E. Meyer, an attractive woman in her fifties and the co-owner of the *Washington Post*, who, having grown up in a German-American family, spoke and wrote German well. She sent him a copy of her interview, printed on the first page, and a letter offering him the *Washington Post* for his publications. Her knowledge of his work impressed him. Meyer had previously befriended the French author Paul Claudel; she loved to be close to famous artists. In May the Manns were back in Küsnacht.

On short notice, in October of the same year, Thomas delivered 'Richard Wagner und der Ring des Nibelungen' (1937; Richard Wagner and the Ring of the Nibelung) as an introductory lecture for a complete performance of Wagner's cycle of musical dramas in the Zurich Opera House. The presentation starts with the assurance that his admiration for Wagner's work could not be diminished, not even touched, by 'any hostile misuse' (*GW* IX, 502; cf. *EL*, 353). Wagner was Hitler's favourite composer.

Katia and Thomas returned to New York on 21 February 1938. On arrival, he issued a press release sharply criticizing the British and French policy of appeasement, their toleration of German rearmament. The Manns planned on staying longer in the USA this time; an agent had arranged a multi-city lecture tour spanning the country. Public lectures were in vogue in the United States before the advent of television, and Mann was well received. Still, lecturing in English was difficult for him, despite rehearsing his pronunciation with Erika and having support during the question-and-answer periods. His presentation, under the title 'Vom kommenden Sieg der Demokratie' (1938; The Coming Victory of Democracy), was aimed at convincing his audience that the seemingly novel approach to building a new society offered by the fascists was misguided.

Mann supported the policies of President Franklin Roosevelt. Democracy offered justice, freedom and truth. He expected it to develop into a democratic socialism and a global order built on the fair distribution of property and raw materials. While one can

Thomas Mann with producers and actors (L–R): Carl Laemmle, Max Reinhardt and Ernst Lubitch in Beverly Hills, 1938.

disapprove of and fear the internal politics in Russia, he assured his listeners, one must recognize Russia as a peaceful nation alongside democracies (*EK* IV, 214–44).[2]

The annexation of Austria in March 1938 made the Manns decide to settle permanently in the United States. During a stay in Beverly Hills, California, Thomas Mann began a reflective essay about his time in exile that he called 'Tagebuchblätter' (Leaves of a Diary). He counters the loss of home and country with a resolution: 'My home lies in the plans that reside within me. Immersed in them, I feel all the warmth of being home . . . Where I am, there is Germany' (*EK* IV, 440). Mann had made a similar statement to reporters on his arrival in New York City. He meant it defensively: the German regime could not take away his Germanness, and he would continue writing in German while living in the United States.

During a lecture tour in Toronto, the Manns applied for American citizenship. By the end of May, they were on the East Coast, spending several weeks in Jamestown, Rhode Island, in a house belonging to an enthusiastic reader. There Mann finished his essay 'Schopenhauer', an introduction to an American selection of Schopenhauer texts. More help came from Agnes Meyer, who had raised funds from several foundations to finance a one-year appointment for him as Lecturer in the Humanities at Princeton University.[3] Katia rented a spacious house for the extended family. Between July and September, the Manns returned to Switzerland and dissolved the household in Küsnacht. The family, including the youngest children Elisabeth and Michael, returned to New York in late September.

During their crossing, conflict developed in the Sudeten region of what was then Czechoslovakia. Hitler, planning to attack the republic, had encouraged a Czechoslovakian political party representing the country's German-speaking minority to demand unacceptable political concessions. The governments of Britain and France, aware that their citizens wanted to avoid war, signed the Munich Agreement to relinquish the German-speaking areas. Mann, now a Czech citizen, addressed a rally in New York's Madison Square. Much applause accompanied his demand: 'Hitler must fall' (Diary, 25 September 1938). His arrival in Princeton at the end of September was overshadowed by the Munich Agreement. Thomas Mann once more raged against the British appeasement policy in the pamphlet 'Dieser Friede' (1938; This Peace).[4] Late November brought the first lecture in Princeton: Goethe's *Faust*, followed by one on his own *Magic Mountain*, and others about Wagner and Freud. Albert Einstein lived near the Manns, and a friendly relationship ensued.

The lecture 'Das Problem der Freiheit' (1939; The Problem of Freedom),[5] written for the second cross-America lecture tour and for the meeting of the PEN club in Stockholm in August 1939, once again expresses Mann's desire that democracy progress towards social justice, while stressing Christian charity. Near the end of the presentation, Mann assures himself: 'We know again what good and evil is' (*EK* V, 74); with this remark he separates himself from

Nietzsche, who had rejected catalogued offences issued by imagined deities as 'slave morality'. All ethics should be geared towards the enhancement of 'Life'. As Mann's lecture 'Nietzsches Philosophie im Lichte unserer Erfahrung' (1947; Nietzsche's Philosophy in the Light of Contemporary Events) will show, it was not a radical departure.

In Chicago, in March 1939, during another lecture tour, with the title 'The Problem of Freedom', the Manns learned that Hitler had forced the dissolution of the Czechoslovak Republic, an event that confirmed their decision to stay in the United States. At this time, Thomas Mann began to question one of his own cultural predilections: Richard Wagner. To be sure, he had criticized Wagner in his recent lectures (1933 and 1937), but he had also called him a great artist, separating his work from the recent misuse. Now, in his response to an article by the historian Peter Viereck, 'Hitler and Wagner', he went a step further. He agreed with Viereck that much in Wagner's music precurses the Nazis' world view and that this view must be defeated. Subsequently, Germany itself must be defeated, because 'there is only *one* Germany, not an evil and a good one.'[6] But his love for Wagner's music was little affected by the new political insight.

The Manns returned once more to Europe, starting in June 1939 before the Continent would be closed to them for eight years. By August they had reached Stockholm, the new location of the Fischer publishing house, now operated by Brigitte Bermann Fischer and her husband, Gottfried. They continued to publish Mann's original German texts. The lecture 'The Problem of Freedom', now scheduled for the meeting of the PEN club during that month, could no longer be given. On 1 September, Germany bombed Warsaw and invaded Poland, starting the Second World War. The Manns managed to fly to London from Sweden and sail from Southampton to New York on the crowded American liner *Washington*.

Having returned to Princeton, Mann completed *Lotte in Weimar* in October and composed the essay 'Dieser Krieg' (1940; This War).

In it he expresses his disappointment with the German people for their support of the war. He offers his thoughts for a peace that would build a new world, a commonwealth of nations dedicated to exercising social democracy in clear opposition to a fascist empire defined by dominance and slavery. His diary reflects his deep depression over the unexpected defeat of France in 1940. Princeton University could offer only an appointment for the spring semester of 1940 with Mann lecturing on 'Goethe's Werther' and 'The Art of the Novel' and 'On Myself', an autobiographical report about his work. The university also had him participate in seminars on 'Tonio Kröger' and 'Faust'. He also resumed travelling with his lecture 'The Problem of Freedom', mostly in support of President Roosevelt, who was re-evaluating the American Neutrality Acts blocking his support of Britain. Earlier that year, in mid-January, Mann had been invited to the White House for a second time.

In July the Manns bought a building site in Pacific Palisades, a suburb of Los Angeles, California. In October, after returning to Princeton, they met their son Golo, brother Heinrich and his wife Nelly in New York. Having escaped from occupied France, they had made their way to the USA through Spain and Portugal with Agnes Meyer helping to secure entry visas. The Mann's fourth child, Monika, had survived the sinking of a British liner by a German submarine.

In October 1940 Thomas Mann began sending written messages to the German people to be broadcast by the BBC. The first message assured his fellow citizens that America stood with Great Britain; Americans, he emphasized, hoped that the German people would end the war. Beginning in March of the following year, the messages were recorded in German, forwarded to England and broadcast from there.

The family left Princeton for California, renting in Pacific Palisades while their home was under construction: the move-in date was February 1942. Many other German-speaking exiles lived in the

Los Angeles area: Heinrich Mann, his friends Bruno Frank and Bruno Walter, the composer Arnold Schoenberg, the writers Franz Werfel and Lion Feuchtwanger, the philosophers Max Horkheimer and Theodor Adorno. There was less contact with the writers Alfred Döblin and Bertolt Brecht, who considered Thomas Mann's socialist leanings insufficient.[7] Hitler sent the German army into the Soviet Union in June 1941; Japan bombed Pearl Harbor on 7 December. America's entry into the war strengthened Mann's faith in the eventual defeat of the Nazi regime. In the autumn of 1941, a lecture tour with anti-fascist messages, 'How to Win the Peace' or 'The War and the Future', covered much of the United States.

Financial concerns were eased by support from Agnes Meyer, who secretly sponsored a position for Mann at the Library of Congress – with an annual stipend of $4,800 – as Consultant in German Literature. He was responsible for no more than a yearly lecture in Washington, DC, with the inaugural one in November 1942 carrying the title 'The Theme of the Joseph Novels'.

After the bombing of Lübeck, Thomas Mann's home town, the BBC demanded a special message from its famous citizen. His first reaction was 'hardly doable' (*kaum tunlich*, Diary, 4 April 1942), but he wrote a speech the next day. 'I think of Coventry, and I have no objection to the notion that everything must be paid up.' He ends with the hope that, after the fall of Hitler, a Germany will emerge that will look to the future of humanity (*EK* V, 180–82). In other radio messages he informs his listeners of the mass murder of Jews.

The entire Mann family was now in the USA. The oldest children, Erika and Klaus, collaborated in publishing anti-fascist books. Klaus edited an intellectual journal, *Decision*, for a year; both were suspected of Communist sympathies by the FBI. During the Blitz, Erika had worked as a war correspondent in Britain and Egypt; Klaus volunteered for the U.S. Army and served in 1944 in a propaganda unit in Italy. Golo, by then a professor of history, joined the U.S. Army in 1943 and became an intelligence officer. Elisabeth lived with her

The Mann family residence in Pacific Palisades, California, in the 1940s.

husband, an anti-fascist Italian professor, and their two daughters in Chicago. Michael, married with two children, played viola and violin in the San Francisco Orchestra. After the catastrophe, Monika lived with her parents and moved with them to California.

Among his four grandchildren, Mann favoured his grandson Frido, who, to Thomas's delight, repeatedly spent weeks with the family in Pacific Palisades. Not all relationships fared as well. The one with his brother had become difficult: when Heinrich's one-year screenwriting contract with Warner Brothers – the sponsor of his visa – expired in November 1941, he and his wife, Nelly, were forced to rely on Thomas for support. The family found Nelly socially unacceptable; she was uneducated and suffered from alcoholism. Late in 1944 she took her own life. Although Heinrich kept in close contact with the family in Pacific Palisades, the relationship remained cool. After the war Thomas encouraged his brother to move to East Germany, where he had been appointed President of the Academy of Arts, but Heinrich died in March 1950.

Following the completion of *Lotte in Weimar*, Mann did not immediately return to the Joseph novels. As recorded in his diary, on 7 October 1939, he had read the summary of a mythical story about transposed heads that was part of an article about the Indian mother of the world, sent to him by the Indologist Heinrich Zimmer.[8] The myth must have reminded him of Goethe's poem 'Paria' the fictive Goethe of his *Lotte in Weimar* had thought about during his monologue, where the goddess acquires the body of a criminal. Mann uses it to play with class prejudices.

In *Die vertauschten Köpfe* (1940; The Transposed Heads), two friends in love with the same woman, Sita, decapitate themselves in despairing jealousy before an image of the goddess Kali. The scene evokes Schopenhauer's philosophy in a humorous manner, when this goddess, speaking to Sita, complains about the prattle of thinkers who declare human existence an illness carried on to new generations by infectious lust (*GW* VIII, 758; cf. *SL* II, 249–50). When the goddess orders Sita to restore the heads to their proper place, Sita mistakenly switches them and places the head of her husband, the more intelligent friend, on the body of the more attractive man. But the change is only temporary. The friend with the more intelligent mind cannot keep his now attractive body; it returns to its former shape. Thereupon, Sita leaves him, rightly expecting that the head of the other friend had regenerated its former body.

Since all three agree that society has no place for them, the friends take each other's lives with their swords, and Sita mounts the funeral pyre. Their honour allows no other way: 'Polyandry does not come into consideration among superior beings' (*GW* VIII, 802; cf. *SL* II, 283). The text ironizes such social honour by describing how it feels to be burned alive: 'If the lovely Sita shrieked awhile – because fire if one is not already dead is frightfully painful – her voice was drowned out by the yelling of conches and the rolling of drums so that it was just as though she had not shrieked' (*GW* VIII, 806; *SL* II, 286). The sentence is characteristic of Thomas Mann's style: his playful irony is serious.

The fairy tale in an Indian setting repeats, in a gruesome way, what had been a subject in all of Thomas Mann's work: the rules of society curtail love. Here Sita is given to her husband without her consent. The tale also plays with the philosophical problem of the relationship between mind (*Geist*) and body: in modernity the traditional dualism competes with monism, the belief in a God of the Whole who is not located in a transcendent heaven. Dissolving the traditional dualism had a political dimension for Mann. In his diary of 19 January 1920, he wishes for a political union of conservative *Bildungsbürger* (representing *Geist*) and workers, meaning the Social Democrats. Citizens with *Geist*, intellectuals, especially those with creative gifts, were to lead ordinary citizens. Joseph's story expressed that desire as well, plus the difficulty of obtaining it. But now, in 1940, the vision had been *verhunzt*, fallen to the dogs in Germany. The tale of transposed heads tells of an intelligent mind who fails to hold on to an attractive body in the way the intellectual *Bildungsbürger*, *Geist*, had failed to rule the body politic. Mann finished *Die vertauschten Köpfe* at the end of July 1940. The German text was published that year, in English a year later.

Joseph der Ernährer (1943; *Joseph the Provider*), the fourth and final volume of *Joseph und seine Brüder*, presents, as the earlier volumes did, lively invented scenes. The narrator playfully asserts that the 'story unfolds here anew in the same way it did in reality' (*FA* VIII.I, 1382; cf. *JW*, 1077, 1209), claiming to have insight into biblical times. The action unfolds with Joseph being transported to jail according to Peteprê's judgement. Our text assures us of Joseph's dignity; he follows his God-ordained destiny. When he arrives at the prison, the warden enquires if he had been Peteprê's former supervisor. Joseph answers, 'I am he' (*Ich bin's*) (*FA* VIII.I, 1366; *JW*, 1065), using the Greek formula for the appearance of a god: 'epiphany'. The same formula, as a reply to an innocent question, occurs several other times. The biblical account does not give epiphanies to Joseph, but Mann's figure alludes to 'the saviour' in Christian theology. The prisoners in jail toil in a quarry, suggesting forced labour in German concentration camps. Joseph, however, rising quickly to a supervisory role, softens the prisoners' fate. When two courtiers, a Count Butler and a Prince Baker, accused of participation in a court conspiracy, arrive in the jail, Joseph treats them with kindness, interpreting their dreams according to Sigmund Freud's dream theory.

Freud, writing his book on the Egyptian Moses and monotheism (*Moses and Monotheism* was published in New York in 1939), had suggested to Thomas Mann during his visit in 1937 that Jacob's monotheism meets the monotheism of Pharaoh Amenhotep IV, who later changed his name to Akhenaten (*BM* II, 22; *LW*, 263). This pharaoh was a religious reformer with modernist intentions. Mann gave Akhenaten's portrait in *Joseph der Ernährer* the weakness that he often attributed to men of the spirit: his pharaoh is subject to seizures and is more peace-minded than is good for the ruler of an empire.

For the theological discussion between Joseph and the Pharaoh, the narrator uses Christian vocabulary: pharaoh is god and man, as the Christian doctrine of Jesus has it and consequently calls his mother 'mother of god' (*FA* VIII.1, 1486; cf. *JW*, 1155). Just as playful is his calling Joseph an 'inspired lamb' (*FA* VIII.1, 1488; *JW*, 1156), alluding to the Lamb of God in Christianity. The Pharaoh's spirituality is countered by Joseph while being supported by Teje, the Pharaoh's mother, who until recently had been regent and is a good politician. Together they bring the seventeen-year-old idealistic pharaoh down to earth.[9]

As Minister of Agriculture, Joseph suggests a controlled economy, taking from the rich and caring for the poor. While this mimics the spirit of Roosevelt's New Deal, it exceeds it: all agriculture is moved under the control of the crown, bearing resemblance to the failed experiments in Communist countries (*FA* VIII.1, 1571–9; *JW*, 1438–47). Thomas Mann's dream of a better social world, however, succeeds in his fiction as it would in a fairy tale: it is popular and works well.

The action returns to Canaan, where Jacob's sons cannot take away their father's suspicion of having had a hand in Joseph's murder, and where Tamar (Mann writes Thamar) learns about the history of Abraham's tribe. This is an occasion for the narrator to play with the improbability of some of the biblical accounts: 'God misspoke at times and did not mean exactly what he was saying' (*FA* VIII.I, 1631; cf. *JW*, 1268). But it is still God who is speaking.

Mann in Pacific Palisades, California, 1941.

Tamar, having been taught by Jacob about the promised future of Abraham's tribe, inserts herself into this future, which the narrator calls the 'history of the world'. Her child Perez, fathered by Judah, will be an ancestor to King David and therefore to Jesus. The text of Mann's novel does not raise doubt that Tamar has rightly succeeded in securing her place in the biblical history of the world. But the reader will ask whether the means she had employed, playing a prostitute and seducing Judah, are worthy of her holy purpose.

The tale of Tamar is inserted into the Joseph story where it does not necessarily belong. It confirms the tendency of *Joseph und seine Brüder* to remove God as an ethical centre from the imagined retelling of Genesis. The biblical God, punishing Onan for spilling his seed, provides another example. Thomas Mann does not involve God at all: Tamar causes Onan's death (*FA* VIII.I, 1646; *JW* 1279). Yet the novel respects the biblical tradition as a value to be honoured regardless of any question of scholarly or scientific veracity.

Judah can be the slave of Astaroth, the goddess of love, who makes him live in 'the hell of sex'. 'Hell,' the text defines, 'is for the pure, that is the law of the moral world' (*FA* VIII.I, 1625; cf. *JW*, 1263), a very modern morality. Judah also still sacrifices to Abraham's God, and he receives Jacob's blessing. He will continue the history of the tribe, his disorderly sex life notwithstanding, his ethical achievement not being chastity itself, but the battle of trying to attain it. In the Joseph novels, goodness does not depend on mastering a set of prescribed rules, but in weighing good and evil after exposing oneself to the latter. Hans Castorp had spoken in similar terms to Clawdia Chauchat in *Der Zauberberg*.

Joseph's 'holy play' (*das heilige Spiel*) with his brothers when they arrive in Egypt becomes a feast of reconciliation. He assures his brothers that their betrayal is forgiven without thought of revenge: 'For, a man, who uses power contrary to justice and reason just because he has it, is a laughing matter. And if he is not yet [a laughing matter], he shall be in the future' (*FA* VIII.I, 1920; cf. *JW*, 1491).

Joseph und seine Brüder had started in 1926 with the hope for a renewed social order. The novel ended in 1943 with the hope that power politics would become a laughing matter for mankind. The last volume, *Joseph der Ernährer*, was finished in January 1943 and published in Stockholm in the same year, the first complete English translation in 1948.

The story 'Das Gesetz' (1944; The Tables of the Law), written immediately after the completion of *Joseph der Ernährer*, was first printed in a collective volume with contributions by ten writers, each showing how one particular commandment of the ten was violated by the German regime. Mann had been asked to write an introduction. Instead, reluctant to moralize, he transforms the events narrated in Exodus into the novella of an artist as leader. Moses forms a people like the sculptor Michelangelo, reducing the active role of God in favour of the artist's work. During the escape from Egypt, the Hebrews steal and murder. Mann's Moses wants to prevent a repetition of the transgressions (*GW* VIII, 829; *SL* II, 307), but his education falls short, as they dance around the golden calf – most likely an Egyptian fertility god. The novella of Moses humanizes the biblical account; miracles find their natural explanations. Mann's Moses chisels the commandments into stone tablets, inventing script as he goes along, while in the Bible God does the writing. Hard-working Moses needs the comfort of a black woman during his labour, and no censure arrives from Yahweh.

Moses is a strong leader. His people regard him as a god when he is successful but abandon him when he fails, making 'Das Gesetz' a political narrative. Moses had to quell the festival of the bull after returning from the mountain carrying the tablets; he had the instigators executed. As a charismatic leader, Moses does not appear to be too different from a dictator. At the end, Mann has him curse the man who invalidated the Ten Commandments, meaning Hitler. The ironic distance that permeates most of the Moses novella ceases at the end where Mann wants to make an unequivocal statement.

While *Joseph der Ernährer* was in the planning stage, Mann travelled widely and presented lectures with titles such as 'War and Democracy', 'How to Win the Peace' or 'The War and the Future'.[10] In November 1942 he delivered the address 'The Theme of the Joseph Novels' in the Library of Congress in Washington, DC, fulfilling his yearly duty as consultant.

The European war had turned a corner in 1943; German exiles in Los Angeles and New York began discussing a Free Germany Committee to represent the German nation, similar to a government in exile. Mann was approached for the position of president, but he made his acceptance contingent upon the U.S. government's encouragement. However, an informal discussion with a friend of the Meyers, Adolf August Berle, an undersecretary in the Department of State (although not for European Affairs), was not reassuring, and Mann wanted to remain loyal to the nation that had given him refuge. He became an American citizen on 23 June 1944; in September and October 1944 he participated in the campaign for the re-election of Franklin Roosevelt with an essay and a speech.

In 1944 German exiles formed a Council for a Democratic Germany. When Mann refused to join or sign its proclamation, Clifton Fadiman, a New York intellectual, asked him to explain his refusal to the public, but he declined. While he had not wanted to accept the role of protector of the German people when they were still fighting a war, he wrote to Fadiman, neither did he want to be their prosecutor, perhaps provoking destructive measures against a country gone astray and now burdened with guilt. Yet he wanted to remain faithful to the German language, in which he aimed to conclude his work.[11]

8

Doctor Faustus and Discord with Germany

On 3 April 1945, only weeks before the capitulation of the German armed forces, Thomas Mann wrote in his diary: 'The German people – bitter disappointment.' Hitler's power was dwindling, yet there were no reports of resistance or uprisings within the country. On 7 May, the day of the final German surrender, he entered: 'Up to now any disavowal of National Socialism is missing, any word that the "seizure of power" was a terrible misfortune, that it was a crime of the first order to have allowed or favoured it.' After the concentration camps had been occupied and the atrocities exposed by American forces, the Office of War Information had asked Mann for a statement to be published in the new, controlled newspapers in the American occupation zone. Mann wrote, 'The torture chamber that was National Socialist Germany lies now open, and the disgrace is exposed for the eyes of the world to see'; he includes himself when he speaks of 'our shame'. Hundreds of thousands of Germans of the so-called elite had committed the crimes in the camps, and ordinary citizens, living next to the places of atrocities, had tolerated them. German power is lost, he concluded, but power is not everything, it is not even the main thing, and German greatness was never a matter of power (*EK* VI, 11–13). The version in a Bavarian publication was titled (not by him): 'Thomas Mann on German Guilt'.

A group of German-speaking American officers under the direction of the Hungarian journalist Hans Habe had taken tutelage of an emerging German press in the American zone of occupation.

The group was tasked with transforming army bulletins, issued for the inhabitants, into a new German press and helping to facilitate contact among exiles and those opponents who had stayed in the country. Habe succeeded in engaging the second group but failed to reconcile German exiles to them. They distrusted one another.

In the lecture 'Germany and the Germans' (*EK* V, 260–81), written during the last days of the war, Mann took on his own German heritage. It was a painful self-examination on 29 May 1945 at the Library of Congress. Again, he insisted there is only one Germany. Its Romanticism, once a reservoir of high-quality art and still loved by him, had rejected enlightened modernity. Lübeck, his birthplace, which, in 1926, he could still praise for its cosmopolitanism ('Weltbürgerlichkeit'; *EK* III, 37), had shrunk to a provincial Gothic town. Martin Luther was a great man, but separating himself and his followers from Roman Catholicism was a blow to Europe and 'the world', his rudeness primitive and repulsive. Mann oddly derives German aggression from what he calls 'Weltscheu', a shyness towards the world that the German *Bildungsbürger* wants to overcome with violence. The multilingualism of small Switzerland contains more 'world', he maintains, than big German cities, adding: 'Not a word of what I have told you about Germany . . . came from alien, cool, objective knowledge; it is all within me. I have been through it all' (*EK* V, 279; cf. *LC*, 64–5). 'Germany and the Germans' is a self-tormenting demonstration of Mann's willingness to change his perspective.

He missed such willingness among defeated Germans when invitations to visit the country reached him. One came from Walter von Molo, a writer who had worked with him in the Prussian Academy of Arts and had read a positive attitude towards Germany in Mann's May statement on the concentration camps. Molo's Open Letter, published in army-controlled German-language papers, asked him to visit Germany and address its suffering people in the name of solidarity. The innermost core of them, Molo maintained, had nothing in common with the Nazis; like a good physician, he should come to heal the sick. Mann received Molo's Open Letter on 10 August 1945, just six days after its publication in Germany. Hans Habe and his group were obviously eager to further their goal of promoting contact between exiles and the disaffected who had remained behind.

But Mann hesitated. He confided his ambivalence to another exile: 'Horror and an inquisitive kind of attachment [to Germany] balance one another.'[1] He did not start composing an answer to Molo until 2 September and did not send it off to the Office of War Information until several days later. Another copy went to *Aufbau*, a German-language weekly published in New York. It was printed there on 28 October, slightly abbreviated, under the title, 'Why I do not Return to Germany'. The title reflects the journal's intent to promote the loyalty of its readers to the country that had taken them in, but it could be misunderstood: Mann had not excluded a visit. In his diary he calls the piece 'Brief nach Deutschland' (Letter to Germany). A few post-war papers developed by Habe published it in early October.

In the answer to Molo, Thomas Mann calls his invitation to return to Germany naive; it ignored the misery and loneliness of exile he and his family had endured. Those who had stayed in the country while continuing to create culture for the regime were the ones who had denied solidarity. Had Germany's elite (the *Bildungsbürger*) declared a strike or left the country, much might have been different. Instead, they stayed, embellishing the murderous regime. Their production, tainted with the smell of blood and disgrace, deserves nothing better than to be pounded into pulp. Yet, while honouring his American citizenship, he will not deny his ties to Germany and will continue to write in German. Eventually, he will visit a Germany that will be a happier place in the new world order (*FA* XIX.I, 72–82). Mann's letter caused disappointment in Germany. The announcement of a potential visit to occupied Germany at the end of the letter was ignored; the refusal to move back permanently was what counted.

German writers and journalists who had published in Germany while secretly opposing the regime now coined the phrase 'inner emigration' (*Innere Emigration*), claiming to be morally superior to exiles who had spent the war under palm trees. Mann despised the inner emigrants; the breach between him and the new German press lingered for a generation, even though his new books were well received.

When he delivered his lecture 'Germany and the Germans' in Washington, DC, Mann had been at work for two years on the novel *Doktor Faustus: Das Leben des deutschen Tonsetzers Adrian Leverkühn, erzählt von einem Freunde* (1947; *Doctor Faustus: The Life of the German Composer Adrian Leverkühn, as told by a Friend*). Ideas for the novel go back to 1904 when Thomas was courting Katia. One has a failing artist fear losing his outsider perspective should he decide to have a family; another envisions a writer suffering from syphilis while pursuing a young girl, taking his life before the wedding (*NB* II, 107). One note identifies the syphilitic writer as a Doctor Faustus whose devil has him infected with the disease. The syphilis bacteria cause intoxication that inspires him to wonderful works until he dies of paralysis (*NB* II, 121–2).

Inspiration achieved by intoxication alludes to Nietzsche's autobiographical essay, *Ecce Homo: How One Becomes What One Is*. A book by the neurologist Paul Julius Möbius, published in 1902 and known by Mann, claims that the euphoric language in *Ecce Homo*, especially in the section where Nietzsche describes his inspiration for *Thus Spoke Zarathustra*, is evidence for a diagnosis of syphilis. Other ideas, recorded between 1901 and 1904 for the planned society novel, became part of *Doktor Faustus*, especially the Adelaide episode, reflecting Mann's love for Paul Ehrenberg. A Faustus novella, evident from occasional entries in the diaries beginning in 1933, remained alive in Mann's imagination, even during the production of the

Joseph novels. One diary entry, of 11 February 1934, speaks of the Faust novella as a symbol for the conditions and fate of Europe. But at the time of the actual writing, beginning in 1943, the German theme had pushed European issues into the background of Mann's consciousness, where they remained.

The fictional narrator of the novel is the Gymnasium teacher Serenus Zeitblom, a well-educated *Bildungsbürger* who had resigned his teaching position when Hitler seized power. The biography of his friend Adrian Leverkühn has the protagonist use his extreme intelligence to compose extraordinary modernistic music assisted by the syphilis bacteria in his brain, a gift from the Devil. The bacteria remove Leverkühn's inhibitions, allowing for his uncompromising modernity.

Zeitblom insists that all things demonic are foreign to his nature, yet he is able to write Adrian's biography because he accepts demonic influences on human life in general (*FA* x.i, 12; *DW*, 6). He loves Adrian, although Leverkühn does not return his feelings; 'interest' is a stronger emotion for the modernist (*FA* x.i, 106; *DW*, 77). But, Zeitblom, the *Bildungsbürger*, does not understand the demonic nature of his friend. He, for instance, accepts Leverkühn's marriage plan at face value, not recognizing it as a Devil-inspired design to punish the violinist Schwerdtfeger for loving Leverkühn.

Wanting to emphasize Leverkühn's deeply Germanic roots, Mann has him grow up on a farm in the countryside. Exposure to culture follows in the town of Kaisersaschern, befriended by his fellow student Zeitblom. Looking back, Zeitblom describes the town as still filled with medieval spirit, its cathedral sheltering the tomb of Otto III, who, as Holy Roman Emperor in Italy, had hated his German origin. While attending the Gymnasium, Leverkühn proves to be exceptionally gifted, soon feeling superior to the general level of instruction. He develops an interest in the order governing mathematics and music, slowly discovering problems in music. At the University of Halle he follows up with theology, expecting it to reveal to him the heart of culture. But he soon discovers comical sides: one of the professors of theology grows into a satire of Martin Luther. Neither Zeitblom, a classical philology major, nor Leverkühn demonstrate Christian faith, much less piety. Adrian calls God 'the thought that eternally thinks itself' (*FA* x.i, 140; cf. *DW*, 103): the theologian does not believe in a personal god. Zeitblom claims to do so; he regards himself as a loyal, though not practising, Catholic.

When Adrian fails to discover the essence of culture in the study of theology, he switches to musical composition, guided by his music teacher from Kaisersaschern, Wendell Kretzschmar. He earns a Doctor of Philosophy at the University of Leipzig on the side, turning himself into a well-educated *Bildungsbürger*. Schopenhauer's philosophy was most likely part of his curriculum and with it the emphasis on music as the highest good, the representation of the all-encompassing 'Will' itself. But the Devil interferes: he subdues Leverkühn's vanity with sexual desire.

While in Leipzig, Thomas Mann has Leverkühn relive an incident Nietzsche experienced as reported by his fellow student, Paul Deussen. Nietzsche, having hired a porter to show him the sights of Cologne, asked for a restaurant at the tour's end. But the porter takes him to a bordello instead, where, surrounded by scantily dressed women, he finds a piano, strikes a few chords and, as Deussen records, flees.[2] Leverkühn repeats the scene in Leipzig; yet before he reaches the piano, one of the prostitutes touches his cheek with her arm. Enamoured, he yearns for her for an entire year before returning to the bordello, where he discovers that she has moved to Pressburg in Hungary (now Bratislava, the capital of Slovakia). He calls the woman Hetaera Esmeralda after an exotic moth depicted in his father's nature book. When he finds her in Pressburg she warns him of her body, but Adrian insists; the infection with syphilis he willingly incurs represents the contract with the Devil. He does not love Hetaera Esmeralda and leaves

Pressburg immediately, transmuting his desire into songs devoted to her. Mutually satisfying sexual love is absent in *Doktor Faustus*.

His desire for the demonic infection makes little psychological sense, but it is needed for the structure of the novel. *Doktor Faustus* is a symbolic work, although clothed mostly, but not entirely, in realistic action. Several seemingly realistic figures are devils: instructor Schleppfuss at the University of Halle, the porter in Leipzig, the devil as shape shifter who had appeared to Leverkühn in the Italian town of Palestrina, and the seducer Saul Fitelberg, who, in his realistic role, is a Parisian concert agent. The second impersonation of the Devil in Palestrina, a music critic resembling Theodor Adorno, promises Adrian help with modern compositions.

Leverkühn's early pieces use poems by the Romantic Clemens Brentano that contrast the harmony of nature with the motif of death. With these poems, he found a new method of composing, explaining to Zeitblom how he had used five notes for a *lied* about a girl of questionable virtue, the five notes signifying 'hetaera esmeralda', the name he had bestowed on the prostitute. The row of five tones could be varied in numerous ways, but it had to remain stable; no note is allowed to be free. The method can be extended to include all twelve tones and half-tones of the musical scale, which makes it nearly identical to Arnold Schoenberg's serial- or twelve-tone method of composition. Zeitblom raises misgivings: does the constellation of a twelve-tone composition not eliminate the composer's freedom? Adrian insists that the composer's choice of the row of tones itself is free. Zeitblom, answering, compares this musical system with a dictatorship born from the revolutionary cry for 'freedom' (*FA* x.i, 279–83; *DW*, 205–8).

Thomas Mann had heard of the twelve-tone method directly from Schoenberg, who lived near the Manns. He also had contact with Igor Stravinsky, who lived in West Hollywood at the time. Stravinsky had achieved international fame for a series of compositions for a Russian ballet, first performed between

1910 and 1913. After that, he adopted a Neoclassical style. Leverkühn's puppet opera could have followed his model.[3]

But it was with the assistance of Theodor Adorno, who also lived in California, that Thomas Mann turned to Arnold Schoenberg's more radical innovation. Adorno provided Mann with the manuscript of the first part of his *Philosophy of New Music*, whose subject is the historic place of Schoenberg's twelve-tone method. Adorno, who sometimes composed music himself, corrected and approved Mann's representations of Leverkühn's musical pieces. His publications also provided the theories for Leverkühn's teacher, Wendell Kretzschmar, the German-American musician who propagated modernism as a necessary historic development. Echoing Kretzschmar and Adorno, Adrian declares the music of the Classical and Romantic periods as finished: 'The work! It is a sham,' he laments. 'Art wants to stop being illusion and games; it wants to become cognition, ultimate knowledge' ('Erkenntnis') (*FA* x.i, 264–5; cf. *DW*, 192–3). Kretzschmar insists that Beethoven's sonata, op. 111, signifies the end of the sonata form. The changing musical taste of composers and audience, thus history, render the determining force for the production and reception of art obsolete. Adorno thinks as a Hegelian, while Mann's philosophers had been the anti-Hegelians Schopenhauer and Nietzsche. Mann does not share the musical modernism that he has Leverkühn produce.

After Leverkühn establishes social contact in Munich, he settles on a nearby farm in a small village, where he is visited by friends from the city, often by Zeitblom, who had found a teaching position in nearby Freising. Because the buildings of the rural retreat are remnants of a former monastery, Leverkühn remains surrounded by medieval architecture, in sharp contrast to the style of his music. His comic opera 'Love's Labour's Lost', using Shakespeare's text, prompts most spectators to leave before the end. After composing songs in English, French and Italian, Leverkühn sets Friedrich Gottlieb Klopstock's German hymn, *Festival of Spring*, to music.

Zeitblom interprets the piece as an expiatory sacrifice to God ('das werbende Sühneopfer an Gott'; *FA* x.1, 387; cf. *DW*, 281). But the piece is ambivalent and not as clear-cut as Zeitblom wants to have it. The hymn praises God for his creation but also finds his destructive potential in a storm.

Klopstock calls Earth no more than a drop at the rim of a bucket; the smallness of the Earth in the universe dislodges God from his heaven. Uncertainty is not drowned out by the hymnic accolades to the Almighty. The reader will distrust Zeitblom's depictions of Leverkühn asking for God's grace, since his symphonic poem, *Marvels of the Universe*, expresses doubt of God's very existence.

At the beginning of the First World War, Leverkühn is busy composing parodies of nineteenth-century opera, especially of Wagner's musical dramas. Pious gestures of marionettes are to raise fervent laughter. The parodies of the art of the previous century suggest an end of an era, as does the war greeted by Zeitblom in 1914 with an enthusiasm similar to that of his author. In 1943, while writing his biography, Zeitblom recognizes his ambitions of 1914 as absurd.

Leverkühn soon conceives his own idea of a breakthrough. The word itself (*Durchbruch*) appears fourteen times in the novel. Leverkühn wants the sophisticated and elitist nineteenth-century Romantic compositions, especially Wagner's, transcended by serene and modest art serving a community that will not 'have' a culture but 'be' one (*FA* x.1, 469; *DW*, 339). Although moved, Zeitblom is discontented. Such an utterance, he feels, does not suit Leverkühn's ambition. His works must not be popular: his intended audience is the *Bildungsbürger*. Leverkühn's final works will speak to a musical elite.

By the end of the war, and after a severe illness unrecognized as syphilitic by his local physician, Leverkühn composes his oratorio *Apocalipsis cum figuris*. It shares its title with a cycle of fifteen woodcuts by Albrecht Dürer. In contrast to the biblical apocalypse, the Revelation of St John, Leverkühn's oratorio does not end with a new heaven, a new earth, a new Jerusalem and a new life, but in an 'abyss that will engulf everything in its hopeless maw' (*FA* X.I, 524; *DW*, 380). It is the kind of conclusion the new music must necessarily offer, since it no longer wants to be mere play or illusion but present a new perception: the end of the age of culture, as Leverkühn sees it. The twelve-tone method of composition varies the basic rows, leaving no chance for escape. Thus the children's chorus at the beginning of the second part of the oratorio, sounding like the icy music of the spheres, is in its musical substance a reprise of the devils' hellish laughter that concludes the first part of the oratorio (*FA* X.I, 549; *DW*, 397).

Zeitblom discusses the mixture of aestheticism and barbarity characterizing Leverkühn's Oratorio, when it is analysed by a group of educated citizens who are aware that the era of Enlightenment and individualism has come to an end. They recognize the future cultural history of Western civilization as moving towards barbarism. These discussions among *Bildungsbürger* demonstrate how unprepared German intellectuals were when it came to defending their culture against the onslaught of National Socialism.

Adrian's compositions slowly become known among lovers of new music. Frau von Tolna, the widowed owner of a large estate in Hungary, encourages and supports public recognition of Adrian's work and finances the printing of his musical scores. Her role is similar to that of Nadezhda von Meck, who supported the composer Pyotr Ilyich Tchaikovsky. Like Nadezhda, Frau von Tolna does not meet her protégé, although she attends every performance. Markers in the text suggest that she might be Hetaera Esmeralda, married perhaps to the late owner of her present estate, but Zeitblom's biography does not confirm such suspicions. Adrian exchanges letters with Frau von Tolna, as von Meck did with Tchaikovsky, and Thomas Mann with his supporter Agnes Meyer. Frau von Tolna's vast estate is at Adrian's disposal. He makes use of this offer only once.

Leverkühn is erotically attracted to Rudi Schwerdtfeger, a violinist, who entreats him to dedicate a violin concerto to him. Leverkühn obliges. In his piece Adrian mixes half-mocked conventional features with modern ones, calling the concerto a 'pious sin' (*FA* X.I, 620; *DW*, 448). Because the conventional elements make it more pleasing, the work becomes a success. Following the first performance, Leverkühn and Schwerdtfeger holiday in Frau von Tolna's manor house, thereafter addressing each other in the familiar. But the Devil in Palestrina had decreed that Adrian is not allowed to love, that superiority and natural coldness are inescapably paired (*FA* X.I, 363; *DW*, 264) and meant to enhance his outsider nature. Hence, Leverkühn must separate from Schwerdtfeger, and he does so in a complicated, novelistic way involving a marriage proposal by Leverkühn and Schwerdtfeger's murder by his female lover. Leverkühn will blame himself in his final confession for the murder. Zeitblom does not question the veracity of Adrian's improbable marriage plans: it is an opportunity for the reader to doubt Zeitblom's reliability as a narrator. The murder in the streetcar was taken from Mann's designs for 'Die Geliebten' of 1901.

As the Devil had predicted in Palestrina, Adrian's syphilitic attacks alternate with periods of creativity and rapid production. It is similar in his life: a happy interval ends cruelly. He loves his five-year-old nephew Nepomuk, who spends time with him during his mother's illness. When the boy dies of painful meningitis, Adrian is severely shaken. Since he has loved the boy despite the Devil's prohibition, he feels responsible for his death. As he complains to the Devil, bearded, his body leaning against the wall, his head tilted to one shoulder – Leverkühn affects a Christ-like image, impersonating a redeemer in reverse – 'I will take back everything that was good and noble, the humane, that what people have fought for, stormed citadels, what people have greeted with cheers, the Ninth Symphony' (*FA* X.I, 692–3; *DW*, 501).[4]

Leverkühn's final work is the cantata *Dr Fausti Weheklag* (*The Lamentation of Dr Faustus*) recording Doctor Faustus's farewell to students and friends on the evening before the Devil will seize him. Constructed as a reversal of the biblical Last Supper, the cantata's basic 'row', replacing what once was a 'theme', corresponds to a text containing twelve syllabi: 'For I die both as a wicked and good Christian.' As a good Christian, the Faustus in Leverkühn's work continues to hope for his soul's eventual salvation, yet his pious neighbour cannot convert him; he refuses, as Jesus had refused the devil (Matthew 4:1–10). Like his composer Leverkühn, he does not want to return to the traditional *Gottesbürgerlichkeit*, a bourgeois way of life in a world ruled by an assumed benevolent creator God (*FA* x.i, 710; cf. *DW*, 514), the God of Jean Buddenbrook. In contrast to Beethoven's Ninth Symphony, Leverkühn's cantata ends with an orchestral movement that seems to express God the creator's mournful lament over his forlorn world: 'I did not will this' (*FA* x.i, 711; *DW*, 515). In the cello's final tone, Zeitblom recognizes Leverkühn's plea for grace gleaming like a light in the night.

Leverkühn celebrates his farewell from his friends, an assembly of Munich socialites, at his home in the country. Zeitblom has invited the guests with the promise of a performance by Leverkühn with him playing parts of his cantata. In an introductory speech, a confession, Adrian tells his audience that he has pacted with the Devil in order to overcome contemporary art's stagnation and self-loathing. Producing worthwhile art under these conditions requires the help of the supernatural; the Devil has been his willing companion, and he now expects his damnation. Although his hard work might be counted in his favour, he lacks the courage to hope for grace.

Adrian's speech contains fairy-tale elements, initially causing his listeners to think of his confession as a piece of poetry. But soon dread prevails, and the Munich friends begin to leave. Leverkühn moves to the piano, he strikes a dissonant chord, utters a wail, embraces the instrument, and falls to the floor as if pushed. Frau Schweigestill, Leverkühn's landlady, takes his head and upper body into her arms. The scene described by Zeitblom suggests the crucified Christ and lamentations of his death as depicted in a pietà.

Zeitblom ends his report withdrawn in his study from where he can hear, and sometimes see, Munich in flames at night. In prefaces preceding the final chapters of Leverkühn's life, he records the news of the defeat of Hitler's Germany. His epilogue, written after the capitulation of the German armed forces, reports Leverkühn's days in insanity, his last years with his mother on the farm of his childhood; the depictions duplicate the end of Nietzsche's life. Zeitblom's voice, fading out in a prayer, asks God's grace for his friend's soul and for his country, but not before equating defeated Germany with the condemned man tumbling towards hell on Michelangelo's canvas in the Vatican's Sistine Chapel.

Doktor Faustus can be, perhaps must be, read as a self-accusation by the author for having participated in the progressive, permanently innovating and thus destructive culture of the individual, lonely outsider artist joined to the profit-orientated capitalist democracy.[5] Leverkühn, the unworldly (*weltscheu*, FA X.I, 194, 240) artist, had the superior mind to become a cultural leader, but he opted to stay in isolation, composing his apocalyptic poems. The outbreak of the First World War prevented Leverkühn's journey to Paris, where his orchestra works were scheduled to be performed (*FA X.I*, 446; *DW*, 323). It is implied that under European influence Leverkühn would have joined Europe's artistic community. He would have continued his cosmopolitan compositions and possibly have broken away from his German devil.

Once, during the war, Leverkühn expresses the idea of a new, conciliatory culture of love that would no longer be individualistic and materialistic (*FA* X.I, 469; *DW*, 339); the concluding sentences of the *Magic Mountain* had evoked a coming era of love (*FA* V.I, 1085;

MW, 854). But the war had fostered an unsound nationalism in all of Europe.

The novel was not completed until the end of February 1947. A year earlier, Mann underwent surgery for lung cancer. He believed that writing the novel had made him ill, but he recovered quickly and without a recurrence. The essay 'Dostojewsky mit Massen' (1945; Dostoevsky in Moderation), an introduction to an American edition of *The Short Novels of Dostoevsky*, had brought another interruption in the completion of *Doktor Faustus*.

Thomas Mann had sent Arnold Schoenberg a copy of *Doktor Faustus* with the inscription: 'To the actual one' (*dem Eigentlichen*), meaning that Schoenberg was the real inventor of the twelve-tone method. But Schoenberg was enraged; he was convinced that Mann would be the one lastly credited with his invention. Even after Mann had a notice added to the end of the novel, confirming Schoenberg's authorship, he harboured a grudge, relenting only shortly before his death in 1951.

Doktor Faustus relegates Nietzsche's 'pathos of distance', the high value placed on the outsider producing high art, to a pact with the Devil. That does not mean Mann abandoned Nietzsche. His lecture 'Nietzsche in the Light of Our Experience' complemented the presentation of 'Germany and the Germans' at the Library of Congress in April 1947. He delivered the lecture in New York, London and, in German, as 'Nietzsches Philosophie im Lichte unserer Erfahrung' at a meeting of the International PEN club in Zurich. He approaches his subject with a mixture of veneration and commiseration ('Ehrfurcht und Erbarmen'), filled with compassion for an overtasked soul, not unlike Hamlet's (*FA* XIX.I, 186; *LC*, 69–70). He recognizes the misuse of some of Nietzsche's thought by the Nazis and criticizes his philosophy for rejecting reason and morality in favour of instinct and undefined 'Life' (*FA* XIX.I, 208–9; *LC*, 88–9). Mann labels *Ecce Homo*, to which Leverkühn's Devil alludes, an 'uninhibited late work' (*FA* XIX.I, 192; *LC*, 75). But he also celebrates

Nietzsche as the 'greatest philosopher of the waning nineteenth century' (*FA* XIX.I, 188; *LC*, 71), praising his work as an example of a philosophy that delivers more than cold abstractions. Having grown from experience and suffering, it represents a self-sacrifice for humanity.

Thomas and Katia Mann limited their European travel in 1947 to London and Switzerland; they did not visit Germany. In 1947, after returning from Europe, Thomas studied for, and wrote, an introduction to a selection of Goethe's works in translation, *The Permanent Goethe*, published in 1948 by Dial Press in New York. The German original appeared separately in the essay collection *Neue Studien* (1948) under the title 'Phantasie über Goethe' (*GW* IX, 713–54). It is Thomas Mann's most detailed study of his favourite author.

His diary entry of 3 August 1945, reacting to the Potsdam Agreement, reveals how much Mann still felt for his former country in spite of the negative tone of *Doktor Faustus*. He was 'shocked in spite of everything' that the victors not only intended to reduce Germany to an agrarian nation but would take away its agrarian provinces. Yet the same entry reflects his effort to view the events from a distance: 'Germany played *va banque* and lost.' Three days later, the diary reports the bombing of Hiroshima: 'The secret came to light.' Thomas Mann seems to have had some knowledge of the 'secret' from his brother-in-law, the physicist Peter Pringsheim. Reluctantly, Mann had sanctioned and supported the war against Nazi Germany, although he was convinced that wars were no longer permissible. Learning about the effects of radiation, he intensified his appeal for peace; a nuclear war would be nothing but sheer horror.

9

A Second Emigration: Tales of Forgiveness and Joy Emerge

Most of Thomas Mann's fellow citizens did not share his vision for a new global order after the war: wide acceptance of humanitarian socialism, continued cooperation with the Soviet Union and the elimination of free enterprise economics. Not surprisingly, he was soon denounced in the United States as a supporter of Soviet Communism, despite his assurances that he fully rejected the oppressive Communist ideology.

Since the postal connection with Germany was now open, Mann found it necessary to placate several friends who recognized themselves in *Doktor Faustus*, not always portrayed to their advantage. A special case was Theodor Adorno, who had talked to friends about his 'co-authorship' with Mann on his novel. A public thank you by Mann could limit Adorno's claim while still doing justice to his contribution. *Die Entstehung des Doktor Faustus: Roman eines Romans* appeared in Amsterdam in 1949, the English translations in London and New York in 1961.[1] Thomas let the story emerge from his diaries.

In 1949 the *New York Times* asked for an article on Goethe in the year of the two-hundredth anniversary of his birth. Mann's contribution appeared in the *New York Times Magazine* in June under the title 'Goethe: Faust and Mephistopheles'; the German original carried the title 'Goethe, das deutsche Wunder' (Goethe, the German Miracle). It was not Mann's heading; he had named the piece 'Die drei Gewaltigen' (The Three Giants) in his diary, perhaps alluding to the three destructive giants appearing in one of the last scenes of Goethe's *Faust*. This title was first used in 1955 in the East German edition of Mann's collected works.

The essay questions the greatness of three renowned Germans who towered over their social environment: Luther, Goethe and Bismarck. Real greatness, Mann is saying, belongs only to Goethe, whom he describes in contradictory terms that would also befit him personally. Goethe is Faust *and* Mephistopheles; he can be nihilistic *or* embrace all that exists. The section on Luther in 'Die drei Gewaltigen' is largely based on Nietzsche's overt prejudices towards Luther; it is more of a caricature in the spirit of 'Germany and the Germans'. The section on Bismarck is more objective though critical.

The year of the bicentenary of Goethe's birth also brought Mann an invitation from the University of Oxford with the promise of a Doctorate of Letters and the request for a lecture. He wrote 'Goethe und die Demokratie' (1949; Goethe and Democracy), presenting it on the way to Europe at the Library of Congress and a number of East Coast colleges.

While visiting the Meyers in Washington, DC, the Manns met Walter Hallstein, a professor of law at the University of Frankfurt, later Permanent Under-Secretary of State in West Germany, who urged him to speak in Frankfurt, Goethe's birthplace. Although reluctant because of recent hostile correspondence and press coverage, Mann agreed; Hallstein's argument that Mann's celebrating Goethe's anniversary would be beneficial to the growth of Germany's democracy convinced him.

At the Library of Congress Mann read his lecture in English, in Oxford later in German and in London in English. The Manns flew on to Stockholm, where they were met by the news that their eldest son, Klaus, had committed suicide in Cannes, France. Both decided that the lecture obligations in the Scandinavian countries should still be met. Mann read 'Goethe and Democracy' in German in Uppsala, Lund and Copenhagen.

In 'Goethe and Democracy' Mann develops the paradoxical idea of a 'democracy' that organizes society in both a humane and authoritarian way. Mann wanted to see democracy not as a system of government but rather as an appeal to the individual social conscience. In Goethe's verses, 'Let man be noble, helpful and good . . . / Let him do the useful and right without growing tired,' he found the 'highest expression of all democracy' (*FA* XIX.1, 635; cf. *LC*, 131–2). Mann's lecture recognized Goethe's aristocratic individualism, his opposition to the French Revolution and his disapproval of democratic representation, but he saw these traits balanced by Goethe's pragmatism, his sympathy with everything living, his reverence for Protestant Christianity – in spite of his anti-Christian paganism – and his appreciation of the United States as a progressive nation.

Hallstein had persuaded Mann to give the speech in the historic St Paul's Church, where he would also accept Frankfurt's 'Goethe Prize'. For Mann's address he recommended the theme of home-coming, side-stepping possible reproaches. Mann followed the suggestion and wrote 'Ansprache im Goethejahr' (1949; Address in the Year of Goethe) while holidaying in Switzerland.[2] A message reached him there that the city of Weimar in Soviet-occupied East Germany had awarded him honorary citizenship. A Weimar delegation visiting Zurich added another honour: the East German National Goethe Prize. He accepted an invitation to speak in Weimar.

Mann delivered 'Ansprache im Goethejahr' in Frankfurt on 15 July 1949 and on 1 August in Weimar. The address sought to counter any impression that he had criticized Germany as a nation in his radio addresses; he had merely aimed at the evil regime. Turning to Goethe, he concludes on an upbeat theme: Faust's attempt of colonization in the last act of part two, praising the protagonist's effort as a social action, a high form of humanism.

The speeches were applauded, but the positive effect was undermined by the need to respond to an Open Letter by a 'Kampfgruppe gegen Unmenschlichkeit' (Task Force Against

Inhumanity) published in several German newspapers. The anti-Communist group asked Mann to request a visit to the concentration camp at Buchenwald while in Weimar, suggesting that such a visit would encourage prisoners there suffering from tuberculosis and starvation. The camp, erected by the Nazi government, was now used by the Russian administration to incarcerate opponents of the East German regime, among them Social Democrats who had resisted the unification of their party with Communists. Thomas Mann replied in haste before departing for Stuttgart, Munich and Weimar: he meant to visit Germany as a whole, he wrote, not wanting to omit residents in the Eastern Zone, and not ask Weimar's authorities for something they could not possibly grant. This answer caused a reaction in the West German press, denouncing Mann's visit in Weimar as legitimizing a dictatorial regime.

On the journey from Rotterdam to New York by ship, Mann began to write a report about his trip for the *New York Times Magazine*, continuing with it at home in Pacific Palisades. He was interrupted by a request from the Zurich social democratic newspaper *Volksrecht* wanting a response to an Open Letter by Paul Olberg, an anti-Communist social democratic journalist based in Sweden. The Swiss paper had forwarded the letter to Mann, planning on printing it alongside his response. Though written with reverence, Olberg criticized the way Thomas Mann had addressed the German people in Frankfurt: he should not have apologized for his exile. Olberg disapproved of his visit to Weimar even more. Responding, Mann insisted on distinguishing socialism from the absolute baseness of fascism. Admittedly, the authoritarian people's state had gruesome features, but it was 'a boon that in it [East Germany] stupidity and impudence finally have to "shut up"' (*das Maul halten*; FA XIX.I, 720). The return trip from Weimar – by car through flagged villages and towns where youths threw flowers at his convoy – soothed Mann's wounded German soul.

The article for the *New York Times Magazine*, titled 'Germany Today: A Famous Exile's Impression of a Ruined, Vanquished Land and an Unchanging People', appeared on 25 September 1949. It summarizes his observations of the German people. If he had to live in Germany now, he says, things would be no different than in 1932. Only a minority of educated or perceptive people would be friendly; most would resent him, calling him a traitor. For them, everything had been better under Hitler and nationalism. Re-education by the occupying powers had failed; the tension between the United States and the Soviet Union was favouring the negative elements in German society, and National Socialism was re-emerging. Granted, the regime in the Eastern Zone was authoritarian, but Mann chose to remember the solicitous reception there rather than the hate letters he had received in West Germany (*FA* XIX.I, 704–17). There is a trace of narcissism in both the answer to Olberg and the travel report. Mann ignored the West Germans' apprehension towards the Soviet army in East Germany. He also ignored how much the West Germans appreciated the return to free enterprise economics after many years of controlled scarcity.

In the summer of 1950 Katia and Thomas planned another journey to Switzerland. On the way he was to give a lecture at the Library of Congress, and there were more invitations from East Coast locations. In a diary note Mann expressed confidence that his address in Washington would become a historic act, exceeding in importance the one in 1930 in Berlin. While the speech in Berlin had warned against Germany's growing fascist movement, the one in Washington would warn against the prevailing anti-Communist ideology in the United States.[3] In a political speech in February of that year, the Republican Senator Joseph McCarthy had brandished a piece of paper, claiming that it contained a list of known Communists in the U.S. State Department. Fear of Communism was not without reason: the Soviets had started building nuclear weapons the year before, and Chinese Communists had won their civil war.

The autobiographical lecture 'Meine Zeit' (1950; The Years of My Life) contains an appeal for peace.[4] It was delivered in Chicago and New York, but Luther H. Evans, the Librarian of Congress, feared that Mann's speech would damage the reputation of the library. Evans had received a dossier with excerpts from Mann's reports about his recent travels, favouring the Communists in East Germany. The material was probably submitted by the Federal Bureau of Investigation, which had started a file on him in 1937. Agnes Meyer, who wanted to keep her protégé out of the limelight, agreed with Evans to 'omit' the lecture this year. Mann could only consent.

The travel to Europe began, as usual, with a visit to daughter Elisabeth and her family in Chicago. More than a thousand people attended his reading of 'Meine Zeit' at the University of Chicago. Readings in New York, Stockholm, Lund, Paris, Zurich and Basel followed. Everywhere Mann supported peace and, as a result, increased suspicion that he sided with the Soviet peace propaganda. He was still apprehensive of German power, and the planned European Coal and Steel Community worried him despite its potential for uniting Europe.

The celebration of Mann's 75th birthday in Zurich brought an overwhelming number of congratulatory letters and delegations, including one from Lübeck. When his wife, who had waited with the news about an impending operation until after the celebrations, entered hospital, Mann withdrew with his daughter Erika to the Dolder Grand Hotel overlooking Zurich. There a young waiter, Franz Westermeier, caught his eye. How much his sexuality was aroused he confessed in his secret diary. While contact was out of the question, he appreciated the return of the desire, last experienced 23 years earlier with Klaus Heuser. He felt it made him complete.

His lecture 'Meine Zeit', even though Mann oddly denied that it is autobiographical, begins with the acknowledgement of how much his literary production was tied to Christian religious feelings: 'If it is Christian to perceive life, one's own life, as guilt, as indebtedness, as discomfort, as something that urgently needs amends, salvage, and justification, then German theologians, who have called me an "a-Christian writer", are not quite right' (*EK* VI, 160). Even if his production might appear to be playful and humorous, he maintains, it exposes awareness of a need for justification.

Thomas Mann has long been judged as an ironic writer for distancing himself from the world. This distance is the 'guilt', he confesses. 'Meine Zeit' ends with his wish for a universal peace conference, for an end to the arms race, for the establishment of a world government.

Mann's support of peace initiatives became more precarious when in June 1950 North Korean troops invaded South Korea, which was under American protection. Since the Soviet Union was absent at the time and could not register a veto, the United Nations voted for military support of South Korea. The United States and 21 other nations landed troops. Mann saw the American engagement, which lasted until 1953, as part of the Cold War.

When returning from Europe in August 1950, the Manns, remembering how threatening the German border had been in 1933, feared being arrested on arrival in the USA. Erika, a British citizen and at this point living permanently with her parents, flew home through Canada. But all three reached Pacific Palisades unscathed.

By the end of November, he had finished *Der Erwählte* (1951; The Holy Sinner), a tale based on the legend of the fictional Pope Gregorius and put into poetic form by the medieval poet Hartmann von Aue. As a young man Mann had learned about Hartmann and his *Gregorius* from Professor Wilhelm Hertz at Munich's Technical University; Hertz had called Hartmann's epic poem a Christian *Oedipus*. Lecture notes by the student Mann had found the brother–sister incest in the story similar to that of Siegmund and Sieglinde in Wagner's *Valkyrie*.[5]

In the *Gesta Romanorum*, the source for Leverkühn's puppet opera, Mann had encountered a naive form of the Gregorius legend

Lieber Herr Professor,
Dank für Ihr freundliches
Gedenken und Ihren Bericht.
Der Schriftsteller hat es heute
schwer wie je, und es gibt
mehr flaue Meeresstille als
glückliche Fahrt — im Äusseren.
Aber ich sehe, Sie lassen sich nicht
entmutigen, üben Geduld und stel-
len Neues her, während die Wahrheit
den das Getane seinen Weg findet.
dass Ihre Strindberg-Forschungen erregen
meine Neugier. Ich bin auch immer
"busy" und werde Doch bleiben
bis ans Ende. Es ist ja unsere
Zuflucht und Erheiterung in einer
sonst quälenden Welt. Zu Ostern
soll mein "Gregorius" herauskommen.
Jetzt führe ich gemächlich den
"Felix Krull" fort.
Gute Wünsche! Ihr Thomas Mann

Thomas Mann's handwriting in his later years.

(*GW* XI, 687–91), leading him to Hartmann's text itself. While Leverkühn used the legend to mock medieval piety, Mann's retelling of Hartmann is more serious. As reader, he must have been touched by the story of an outsider who severely atones for transgressions he could not have avoided, but which are nevertheless attached to him as 'objective' sins, and by the fairy-tale ending that rewards the sinner with a position enabling him to solve the problems of his world.

Thomas Mann lets Hartmann's story be written down by the Irish monk Clemens while he visits the monastery of St Gallen in Switzerland. Clemens upholds the rules of his Church: incest is a solid sin, and sexual desire is born of the Devil (*GW* VII, 160; *HL*, 206). When God's law is violated, the violator must be punished, no matter the cause of the violation. The narrator tries to convince himself and the reader again and again how hideous incest between a mother and her son is, even though neither son nor mother could have known of their relationship. The narrator's credence turns into playfulness when he tells the reader that the spirit of narration, which rings the bells of Rome that express the grace of God descending on Gregorius, is the narrator Clemens, the Irishman, himself. Most stirring, and inviting the reader's protest against the narrator's concept of sin, is the decision of the knight Eisengrein that the child, born of incest, must disappear because he does not fit into the social order. The child is torn from the arms of his mother, set adrift in a barrel heading out to sea in the dim hope that God will rescue him.

Humorous opposition to the moral rigidity of the Church breaks through in the description of a Roman garden where Probus, the layman, has his vision. Laurels grow and wildflowers bloom amid broken remains of ancient Roman statues of Pan, the god of nature, and Amor (Cupid), the god of love, whose antique statue has lost his head (*GW* VII, 198; *HL*, 256). In medieval Rome Judeo-Christian spirituality rules against nature and sexuality.

The scenes on an island in the English Channel belong to the realistic aspect of the piece. Gregorius, who does not fit into the community of fishermen, replays Tonio Kröger's detachment from ordinary people; he is of a different nature. Can that be guilt? This is the serious question that lingers under the lighter surface of the story.

The scenes when layman Probus and clergyman Liberius travel to the northern lake and rock where Gregorius does his penance are humorous. When they find him, shrunken and resembling a hedgehog, the prelate Liberius, fearing embarrassment for the Church, will not take the subhuman creature to Rome as a future pope. His lay companion insists on continuing the fairy tale and wins. At the end, Sibylla and Gregorius interpret their lives and their reunion as art: 'We thought to offer God entertainment' (*GW* VII, 257; *HL*, 332).

Der Erwählte was published 1951 in German and English. At the end of December 1950, Mann had gone back to work on his novel about the confidence man, *Bekenntnisse des Hochstaplers Felix Krull*, which he had started in 1910 and had set aside in 1913. We will discuss it at the end of this chapter.

On the first day of 1952, the last year the Manns were to spend in the United States, Thomas wrote a statement of his religious belief. The Columbia Broadcasting System had asked for a contribution to its series of broadcasts titled 'This I Believe'. Mann's religious confession appeared in print covered by the headline (not by him) 'Life Grows in the Soil of Time'.[6] He gave the title 'Lob der Vergänglichkeit' to the German original (Praise of Transitoriness; *EK* VI, 219–21).

Transitoriness, the essay argues, is not sad, since time bestows value and dignity on life. Time enables creativity and all sense of progress; it enables us to give soul to things. The awareness of transitoriness, of the beginning and end of life, distinguishes humanity from nature. The human species is a great experiment:

its failure, through the fault of people, would mean a failure of creation itself. The essayist employs the passive voice, avoiding naming a creator. It is remarkable that Mann here labels timelessness – the *nunc stans*, Schopenhauer's eternal now – as 'absolutely uninteresting' (*EK* IV, 219). Schopenhauer's world where the timeless 'Will' rules seems to have fallen away. Mann values his humanism more highly than the 'intellectual organization of the world', as his essay of 1938 had labelled Schopenhauer's philosophy (*EK* IV, 253; *EL*, 372). Since the author of the Joseph novels takes God as the Whole, only He can be the unnamed experimenter of 'This I Believe'.

Asked by the BBC's Third Programme for a contribution to a series of radio essays under the theme 'The Artist and Society', Mann produced an essay that was broadcast in May 1952. He presented its German original, 'Der Künstler und die Gesellschaft' (Artist and Society; *EK* VI, 222–35), as lectures in Europe. The essay portrays the artist as an outsider who nevertheless takes his place in society. The artistic spirit can reside on the political left or right: Knut Hamsun and Ezra Pound, for instance, are found on the right. Fascists had driven Mann to a left-leaning political philosophy, but he assures his readers that he has never lost sight of the comical aspect of his role as itinerant orator for social democracy. He sees his place in the centre of society and does not want to be labelled a leftist.

Early in 1952 Mann had doubts, not for the first time, as to whether he should devote the last years of his life to the fictional biography of a confidence man. Looking for a more dignified subject, he soon found one: at breakfast on 6 April (writing in his diary), he observes his wife reminiscing about an older aristocratic woman in Munich who had fallen in love with the tutor of her son. The woman, believing that her newfound desire has rejuvenated her, finds her belief confirmed when menstruation seemingly returns. But the cause of the bleeding is cancer of the uterus. A few weeks later, after finishing the chapter containing the visit to the Museum of Natural Science in Lisbon, one of the last chapters of the Krull

Thomas Mann in Erlenbach, Zurich, *c.* 1953.

novel's fragment, Mann's diary reports studies for a story of
'the betrayed woman'. The German title of the new novella will
be 'Die Betrogene' (1952). Since a literal translation of the title as
'The Betrayed Woman' was not congenial enough for the American
publisher, it is known in English as 'The Black Swan' (1954), named
after an incident in the story where a black swan jealously hisses
at the woman. We will discuss this text, somewhat resembling
a testimonial by Mann, at the end of this chapter.

When Erika Mann's application for a re-entry permit to the U.S. was denied, the family's permanent return to the United States was out of the question; Erika had become a necessary assistant to her father. Leaving New York in June 1952, they travelled for months in Switzerland, Austria and Germany. In the Dolder Grand Hotel above Zurich, Mann composed a memorial lecture for Gerhart Hauptmann and delivered it in Frankfurt am Main in November. By the end of December, the family moved into a rented house in Erlenbach on Lake Zurich. In October of the following year, the house in Pacific Palisades was sold, enabling the Manns to buy their home in Kilchberg near Zurich in 1954. The German government acquired the California residence in 2016.

During a visit to Rome at the end of April 1953, Mann enjoyed a special audience with Pope Pius XII. He called the encounter in his diary a strong and moving experience. The pope had greeted his visitor standing, speaking to him for fifteen minutes about Rome and his love of Germany. Mann remembered: 'I did not kneel before a human being and politician but before a white, spiritual, mild idol, who represents two occidental millennia' (Diary, 1 May 1953). The honour was followed up by a doctoral degree from the University of Cambridge; readings from *Bekenntnisse des Hochstaplers Felix Krull* were well received in Hamburg, Cologne and Düsseldorf, while the relationship with Germany grew less bitter. For Katia's seventieth birthday in 1953, her husband composed a moving speech, expressing his gratitude for her 'heroic patience, which love and loyalty forced on her natural impatience' (*EK* VI, 251).

Mann's late political utterances confirmed his loyalty to the Western world and continued to plead for peace. The American influence in Europe worried him, most of all the West German government's joining of NATO, but he largely supported the policies of the Social Democrats. Not believing the news accounts of the West German press, he gravely misunderstood the uprising of 17 June 1953 in East Berlin as having been provoked by West Germans

(Diary, 19 and 26 June 1953). Little connection developed with young German writers in West Germany, even though some had leftist orientations. An exception was Alfred Andersch, who appreciated Mann's prose and his politics.

Since he had decided to discontinue the impostor Krull's career, he began to put down notes for a novella or drama on the theme of Martin Luther's wedding. But he had to concentrate first on research for an essay about Friedrich Schiller commemorating the 150th anniversary of his death. 'Versuch über Schiller' (1955; On Schiller) became an essay of ninety pages, of which only an excerpt could be presented as a lecture. The excerpt was broadcast from Stuttgart on 8 May, was well received in all of Germany, and repeated in Weimar on 15 May; the visit to the German Democratic Republic raised less negative publicity this time. Lübeck followed Weimar, where the author of *Buddenbrooks* became an honorary citizen.

Mann's eightieth birthday was celebrated in Zurich in 1955. The President of the Swiss Confederation congratulated him; the feast lasted all day. Afterwards, the Manns spent time in Noordwijk aan Zee in the Netherlands enjoying a seaside holiday. Queen Juliana invited them for a talk in her palace at Soestdijk. On 22 July Thomas experienced leg pain, diagnosed as thrombosis. After being transported to Zurich, there was initial healing, but on 12 August one of his arteries ruptured, causing his death.

We still have to discuss the fragment of *Bekenntnisse des Hochstaplers Felix Krull* and 'Die Betrogene', the novella of the woman encountering a hissing black swan. The Krull novel was originally conceived as a complement to *Königliche Hoheit*. Both protagonists, the prince and the impostor, lead lives of representation; both can playfully suggest the problems of an outsider artist. And yet they occupy opposite ends of the social order.

After 1900, German newspapers had reported the accomplishments of the international impostor Georges

Thomas Mann receiving the Honorary Citizenship of Lübeck in 1955. To either side are Katia Mann and Lübeck's Mayor, Otto Passarge.

Manolescu, who, with great skill and remarkable discipline, had been able to enrich himself, even winning over women of nobility. Thomas Mann studied his memoirs after they appeared in 1905 in German. The autobiography of an artistic criminal offered the opportunity for parodies of famous autobiographies, above all Goethe's *Dichtung und Wahrheit* (*Poetry and Truth: From My Own Life*), but the novel fragment became more than a mere parody.

When Mann started writing in 1910, he chose the son of a tradesman as his confidence man who resisted school even more than his author had. But Krull is class conscious; he strives to have his language sound Goethean by using lofty reflections on life and humanity, often producing a comical effect. We encounter Krull in the beginning of the memoir living in retirement in England after having served years in prison. His crimes, arrest and his serving time in jail were set aside for later parts of the novel. Krull displays his mastery of self-discipline when he simulates an epileptic seizure during a physical examination for military service. Mann enjoyed reading the scene publicly and did so often. It caricatures the militarization of life in the Wilhelminian era, as in 'Ein Glück' (A Gleam) of 1903, where noble cavalry officers are exposed, paralleling brother Heinrich's satire of life under Wilhelm II in *Der Untertan* (*The Man of Straw*).

Early parts of the manuscript, written between 1910 and 1913, break off during Krull's apprenticeship with the prostitute Rozsa, while he is still on the lower end of criminality. His theft of a jewellery case during a customs inspection on the way to Paris does not raise pangs of a guilty conscience with Krull; morality does not hinder his career. There is a touch of social criticism surrounding Krull's service as a Parisian waiter, in line with Thomas Mann's socialist tendencies. Soon, however, Krull will be able to perform in the high-class style, having developed a perfect mode of deception. His success in doing so may sometimes strain the reader's willingness to follow, but the effect is always comical.

Among the scenes that enliven Krull's 'confessions', the sexual encounter with Madame Houpflé is a gem. The scene contributes to one of the themes of the novel: the arbitrariness of class difference. Wealthy author Diane finds sexual satisfaction in humiliating herself by having intercourse with a lift boy. While Krull satisfies Diane, he has to comfort two frustrated lovers: Eleanor Twentyman, the teenage daughter from a wealthy family who is obsessed with him, and Lord Kilmarnock, a homosexual whose offer to live with him Krull rejects. The author gave Kilmarnock his own conspicuous nose.

Near the end of the fragment, Krull learns about life and being from Professor Kuckuck, a palaeontologist and director of the Museum of Natural History in Lisbon. Something must have been added to the mix, the professor teaches, when being arose from nothingness, life from being, and man from animals (*FA* XII.I, 312–13; *CL*, 271). Love, sexual satisfaction, is inseparable from the Whole of Being. Kuckuck has a word for the veneration of this entirety:

'Universal Sympathy' (*Allsympathie*; *FA* XII.1, 319; *CL*, 295). His sympathy for the whole puts a happier face on Schopenhauer's all-encompassing 'Will'. Kuckuck's teachings are close to his author's world view; they include his praise of transitoriness.

Kuckuck's elaborations on 'Universal Sympathy', and his later elucidation of bullfights as derived from ancient and violent religions, cast him as a teacher of religion. Krull still maintains his false identity, but the development of the impostor seems slowed in favour of a novel of education. The reader forgets about listening to a criminal when Krull talks about the miracle of love transforming the separate feeling of two individuals. When Krull wins the love of an adult Romanesque woman, she may resemble Mann's own Portuguese grandmother, whom he never knew.

Mann chose the Rhenisch town of Düsseldorf as the setting for 'Die Betrogene' (The Black Swan). It is the home town of Klaus Heuser, whom Thomas had loved in 1927 around the time of the novella's action. Another such love incident, or 'visitation', had happened to him more recently: the encounter with Franz Westermeier in 1950 in Zurich. The experience of a new love that he had to forgo underlies the story.

The narrator portrays Rosalie von Tümmler, the betrayed woman, as a member of the German middle class. She represents an ordinary burgher who lives in harmony with her daughter, a well-educated modern painter, an artistic *Bildungsbürger*. The action develops at a time when Mann was still confident that *Bildungsbürger* could be drawn into a world view of social harmony, guided by a religion of life that included 'sympathy with death'. The fifty-year-old Rosalie experiences her 'visitation' by falling in love with a much younger man. Similar to the 'visitation' Herr Friedemann encounters, Rosalie's ends with her death, but it is not preceded by rage and humiliation, as was Friedemann's. Rosalie dies reconciled with life, with the All-Being, because she has experienced real, though unfulfilled, love. Despite having been a wife, she has felt love for the first time: 'It is I who desires,' she exclaims (*GW* VIII, 901; cf. *SL* II, 369).

She declares her love in the secret chamber of a Rococo castle during a visit to the site with her family and her beloved, her son's young American tutor. Approaching the castle, the group encounters a flock of black swans in the moat. Rosalie feeds them with bread the young man had carried in a pocket on his body. She also eats some of it herself, suggesting a symbolic union with her beloved, calling to mind the offerings of a religious sacrifice. While Rosalie enjoys watching the beautiful swans, one of them, eager to get to the food, charges toward her, hissing aggressively. His jealous eagerness to reach the food parodies Rosalie's desire, linking it to Schopenhauer's 'Will', to her death and to her acceptance in the Whole of Being.

Rosalie suffuses her death with her new love. We can read her last words to her daughter as a mature religious testimony that stands for the author and is directed to his readers. A symbolic testimonial is also the young American's critique of the United States, raising the possibility of an America different from the one the deeply disappointed author had just left. In 'Die Betrogene' Mann bestows this hope on the young American by having him express the dissatisfaction with his homeland in the strongest terms. He finds it 'appalling' with its 'pursuit of the dollar and insensate church-going', its 'worship of success' and its 'colossal mediocrity'. He prefers history-conscious Europe, perhaps meaning to imply that people could learn from history (*GW* VIII, 897; *SL* II, 365). Although injured in the war against Germany, he feels attracted to a widow of the same war, making her feel genuine love for the first time. Their emotional bond symbolizes the love that should have risen from the 'world festival of death' (*FA* V.1, 1085; *MW*, 854). Mann started the story 'Die Betrogene' in 1952 in Pacific Palisades, California, and completed it in Erlenbach on Lake Zurich in 1953.

Afterword: Modern Perspectives

Much, if not all, of Thomas Mann's fiction carries symbolic meaning. *Buddenbrooks* examines the inhumanity of modern businessmen under the storyline of a declining family. *Fiorenza* lets modern aestheticism fail as a substitute religion, while a priest uses religion to win power for himself. *Der Zauberberg* gives an ordinary young German Romantic freedom to probe modernity, but his freedom *is* Romantic; it is associated with death and with the past. It does not provide the young man with guidelines for the future, leaving him confused and disorientated before he loses himself in the war. 'Wälsungenblut', using the theme of Jewish assimilation, problematizes the role of the outsider when he abandons his isolation, grows wealthy and complacent, while forsaking his artistic calling. *Doktor Faustus* uses the fictional biography of a composer to demonstrate how the ambitions of modern artists can grow destructive and signal the end of an age when art could give comfort in life's struggle after religious certainty had waned. *Der Erwählte* turns against the negativity of *Doktor Faustus* by letting the spirit of narration maintain itself against the narrator's moral order.

Is it irony when Thomas Mann's fiction suggests symbolic undercurrents that open a wider meaning? The word 'irony' appears in *Betrachtungen eines Unpolitischen* in a great variety of shadings. It has encouraged critics to speak of irony as a specific language inhabiting Mann's work. Instead, we propose that Mann employed

Nietzsche's concept of perspectivism, sharing the conviction that all meaning depends on the observer's point of view, and that a metaphysical truth cannot be determined. While irony may use false words to aim at a truth, it holds on to one definitive truth. Perspectivism lets several partial truths convene.

A sudden change of perspective in 'Gladius Dei' helps us to recognize that the term 'perspectivism' is more useful than irony if we wish to understand the modernity of Mann's writing. The narrator observes and describes Hieronymus in early twentieth-century Munich, in a monk's garb, resembling Girolamo Savonarola. The narrator does not seem to have access to Hieronymus's psyche when his figure listens to students describing the picture of a Madonna in a display window. But the perspective suddenly changes: the narrator disappears, and the reader is allowed to enter into Hieronymus's mind where the sensual image of the Madonna has firmly lodged itself. He cannot expel it until a voice from God orders him to intervene against 'frivolous wickedness and the brazen arrogance of beauty' (FA II.1, 230–31; DN, 92). The next chapter narrates Hieronymus's vain action in the store in a dramatic scene: we can follow his words, but the narrator has returned, blocking all insight into his feelings until, in the last paragraphs, Hieronymus's mind comes alive again for the reader.

The change has the effect that neither perspective can lay claim to truth: the order from above is not verified by the narrator's voice. Since Hieronymus's undertaking in the store proves futile, the voice from above is powerless; its existence becomes doubtful. There is no privileged truth. The command from above could be identified as Hieronymus's inner voice, which would make the narrator's inability to access his fictional character's consciousness ironic. But the text does not show preference for either; our insight into Hieronymus's consciousness remains limited, and with it the meaning of the entire text. Our view of Hieronymus becomes ambivalent.

The narrator, in the role of the observer, makes us aware of the inferior quality of the art objects in the 'beauty store' without having to cast judgement. Hieronymus ends as a weakling, unprotected by his God and not revenged by him, madly imagining burning artistic vanities, as Savonarola had done four centuries earlier in Florence. His expectation that the Sword of God will come over Munich is mere imagination. And yet the reader may admire Hieronymus's courage and agree with his message. Is he not right in accusing seductive but inauthentic art as the improper kind of artistic modernity?

In *Der Zauberberg* two characters offer opposing perspectives of their world views: Settembrini and Naphta. A similar pair had appeared at the beginning of *Buddenbrooks* where the older Buddenbrook, a man of the Enlightenment, examines eight-year-old Tony's knowledge of Martin Luther's Small Catechism. He intends to mock Luther's account of creation, teasing Tony's Christian parents. The text makes his point: Tony gets stuck reciting Luther's explanations. On cue from her mother, she happily finds the right words, comparing her rediscovered aptitude with sledding downhill in winter. Tony's exercise has been mere rote learning. The teachings of Christianity are memorized, but the meaning behind them has vanished. The Christian religion, as understood in the bourgeois age, is questioned elsewhere in *Buddenbrooks*. So is an attempt at a substitute religion centred on Schopenhauer's view of death as a return to the 'Will'. The comfort it brings to Thomas Buddenbrook does not last. Religion is an open question in much of Thomas Mann's work. His four-part *Joseph und seine Brüder* traces the development of the highest God among others to the God of the Whole; it is a God who embraces good as well as evil.

The *Joseph* novel deserves to be called Mann's principal work to a greater extent than *Doktor Faustus*, which is severely burdened by the German catastrophe. Mann lets Zeitblom, who has much in common with his author, pray to his personal God, but when speaking of his own religion Mann hesitates to express a personal belief in a living God who issues eternal rules and judges every human being individually. Yet he denounces the intention of the German National Socialists to do away with religion and houses of worship by declaring Christianity, together with the civilizations inherited from antiquity, indispensable elements of Western culture (*FA* XXIII.I, 620).

In the work of James Joyce, we find a similar struggle between a new freedom from binding conventions and the fear of being excluded from the familiar world, of being condemned to be an outsider. Both Joyce's and Mann's fictional works are largely transformed autobiography, showing an externalized inner struggle between the loyalty to familiar ground and the desire to be free to transform it.

References

1 Thomas Mann, the Outsider Writer, in the Shadow of his Brother

1 Ulrich Dietzel and Rosemarie Eggert, eds, *Heinrich Mann, Briefe an Ludwig Ewers, 1889–1913* (Berlin, 1980), p. 343. Heinrich's first novel, *In einer Familie* (1894), was unsuccessful.
2 Ibid., p. 202.
3 Ibid., pp. 106–9, 195.
4 Letter of 25 June 1895: Thomas-Mann-Archive of the Swiss Federal Institute of Technology, Zurich.
5 Helen Lowe-Porter (*SL* I) chose the title 'The Dilettante'; David Luke selected 'The Joker' (*'Death in Venice' and other Stories by Thomas Mann*, trans. David Luke (New York, 1988)).
6 Hans R. Vaget, 'Thomas Mann und Theodor Fontane: Eine rezeptions-ästhetische Studie zu "Der kleine Herr Friedemann"', *Modern Language Notes*, XC (1975), pp. 448–71.
7 Helen Lowe-Porter (*EL*) translates *Weltgrund* as 'universal foundations'.

2 From *Buddenbrooks*, a Novel of Liberation, to *Fiorenza*, a Play of Power

1 These words occur also in the draft of a long letter to Thomas of December 1903. Peter Stein, ed., *Heinrich Mann, Essays und Publizistik: Kritische Gesamtausgabe* (Bielefeld, 2013), vol. I, p. 459.
2 In his autobiographical essay *Ein Zeitalter wird besichtigt* (*An Era is Visited*), composed in 1942–3 in his California exile (Berlin, 1973,

pp. 217–18, 226), Heinrich Mann speaks of his contribution
to *Buddenbrooks* and a plan of writing something together
(not specifically mentioning *Buddenbrooks*). In a letter to
Heinrich, written 18 February 1905, Thomas mentions a
satirical novel about Lübeck with family members as characters
(*FA* XXI, 314).

3 In the Thomas-Mann-Archive of the Swiss Federal Institute of
Technology, Zurich.

3 Two Loves and their Literary Outcomes

1 Cor. XIII:1. Luther's translation uses 'love' ('Liebe'), where the King
James version says 'charity'.

2 Inge and Walter Jens, *Frau Thomas Mann: Das Leben der Katharina
Pringsheim* (Reinbek, 2003), pp. 32–4.

3 Heinrich Mann, *Novellen: Zweiter Band* (Berlin, 1978), pp. 249–60;
see p. 441 for the dedication.

4 'Death in Venice', the First World War and *The Magic Mountain*

1 Katia Mann's remembrances in Katia Mann, *Meine ungeschriebenen
Memoiren* [My Unwritten Memoirs], ed. Elisabeth Plessen and
Michael Mann (Frankfurt/Main, 1974), p. 71.

2 Manfred Hahn, Anne Flierl and Wolfgang Klein, eds, *Heinrich Mann,
Essays und Publizistik: Kritische Gesamtausgabe* (Bielefeld, 2012), vol. II,
pp. 130–32.

3 A translation is in LR, 269–71. The German text is in Ehrhard Bahr,
Thomas Mann, Der Tod in Venedig, Erläuterungen und Documente
(Stuttgart, 2005), pp. 136–8. The immense amount of criticism about
'Der Tod in Venedig' is presented and edited by Ellis Shookman in
Thomas Mann's Death in Venice: A Novella and Its Critics (Rochester,
NY, 2003).

4 Heinrich Mann, *Essays und Publizistik*, p. 199.

5 Mann destroyed his diaries up to 1933 in May 1945; he kept the diaries
for 1918–21 for the composition of *Doktor Faustus*. All references appear

in the text. Peter de Mendelssohn, ed., *Thomas Mann: Tagebücher 1918–1921* (Frankfurt/Main, 1979); *Tagebücher 1933–1934* (Frankfurt/Main, 1977); *Tagebücher 1935–1936* (Frankfurt/Main, 1978); *Tagebücher 1937–1939* (Frankfurt/Main, 1980); *Tagebücher 1940–1943* (Frankfurt/Main, 1982). Inge Jens, ed., *Tagebücher 1944 to 1. 4.1946* (Frankfurt/Main, 1986); *Tagebücher 28.5.1946–31.12.1948* (Frankfurt/Main, 1989). *Tagebücher 1949–1950* (Frankfurt/Main, 1991); *Tagebücher, 1951–1952* (Frankfurt/Main, 1993); *Tagebücher 1953–1955* (Frankfurt/Main, 1995).

6 Diary, 12 November 1918.

7 The diary recorded his participation in the election for the Bavarian State Assembly on 12 January 1919. He voted for the Bayerische Volkspartei, a party of the middle class favoured by most Bavarians. The diary does not record his choice of party for the National Assembly.

8 Friedrich Eicken, *Geschichte und System der mittelalterlichen Weltanschauung* (Stuttgart, 1887).

9 Georg Potempa, ed., *Thomas Mann: Beteiligung an politschen Aufrufen und anderen kollektiven Publikationen* (Morsum/Sylt, 1988), pp. 27–8; Diary, 8 June 1919.

10 See letter to Erich Koch-Weser of 18 December 1928 (*FA* XXIII.I, 374): Mann considers Bolshevism as a corrective principle 'weltwichtig und weltbestimmend' (important and determining for the world's fate).

11 Judith Marcus, *Georg Lukács and Thomas Mann: A Study in the Sociology of Literature* (Amherst, MA, 1987).

12 Letter to Samuel Fischer, 22 August 1914. The letter is not accessible in its entirety. It is partially published in Hans Wysling and Marianne Fischer, eds, *Dichter über ihre Dichtungen: Thomas Mann*, vol. I (Munich, 1975), pp. 453–4.

13 That the narrator, speaking for the author, has Nietzsche in mind without naming him is made clear by Mann's address in 1924 on the occasion of Nietzsche's eightieth birthday (*FA* XV.I, 791).

5 The Weimar Republic and Two *Joseph* Novels

1 See Manfred Dierks, 'Thomas Mann's Late Politics', in *A Companion to the Works of Thomas Mann*, ed. Herbert Lehnert and Eva Wessell (Rochester, NY, 2004), especially pp. 212–16.

2   *Die Geschichten Jaakobs* (1933; The Stories of Jacob), *Der junge Joseph* (1934; Young Joseph), *Joseph in Ägypten* (1936; Joseph in Egypt) and *Joseph der Ernährer* (1943; Joseph the Provider).

3   Alfred Jeremias, *Das alte Testament im Lichte des Alten Orients* (Leipzig, 1904). Thomas Mann used the edition of 1916. His copy is preserved in the Thomas-Mann-Archive of the Swiss Federal Institute of Technology, Zurich. It shows intensive use.

4   Mimekor Yisrael, *Classical Jewish Folktale*s (Bloomington, IL, 1976); *Die Sagen der Juden, collected by Micha Joseph Bin Gorion* [i.e. Micha Josef Berdyczewski] (Frankfurt/Main), 1919.

5   For the interior dialectic of the work see Peter Pütz, 'Joseph and his Brothers', in *A Companion to the Works of Thomas Mann*, ed. Lehnert and Wessell, pp. 159–79.

6 Joseph and his Author in Exile, *Lotte in Weimar*

1   Our source is an interview which Klaus Heuser granted to Karl Werner Böhm. It is printed in Böhm's *Zwischen Selbstzucht und Verlangen: Thomas Mann und das Stigma Homosexualität* (Würzburg, 1991), pp. 377–81.

2   Felix Theilhaber, *Goethe: Sexus und Eros* (Berlin, 1929).

3   For Theilhaber's effect on Mann, see Hinrich Siefken, *Thomas Mann: 'Ideal der Deutschheit'* (Munich, 1981), pp. 230–33; Werner Frizen in *FA* IX.II, 10, 119–21; and Herbert Lehnert in *FA* XIX.II, 399–401.

4   Theilhaber, *Goethe*, p. 288. H.E.R. Belani [pseudonym for Karl Ludwig Häberlin], *Goethe und sein Liebeleben* [*sic*]: *Historischer Novellenkreis* (Leipzig, 1866), vol. II, pp. 223–4.

5   Siefken, *Thomas Mann*, pp. 199–243. H. Siefken, 'Lotte in Weimar – "Contactnahme" and Thomas Mann's Novel about Goethe', *Trivium*, XIII (1978), pp. 38–52. H. Siefken, 'Thomas Mann's Novel "Lotte in Weimar" – a "Lustspiel"?', *Oxford German Studies*, XI (1980), pp. 103–22.

6   See Johann Wolfgang von Goethe, *The Sufferings of Young Werther*, trans. Stanley Corngold (New York, 2012), p. 77. The passage expresses Werther's desire for possessing Lotte in another life. Mager selected a moment in the story that is indeed crucial. See Thomas P. Saine,

'Passion and Aggression: The Meaning of Werther's Last Letter', *Orbis Litterarum*, XXXV (1980), pp. 327–56.

7 Johann Wolfgang Goethe, *West-Eastern Divan*, trans. John Whaley, intro. Katharina Mommsen, bilingual edn (New York, 1998), pp. 348–93.

8 Ibid., pp. 34–5.

9 Ibid., pp. 46–7.

7 In America: The Second World War and *Joseph the Provider*

1 Thomas Mann, *Order of the Day: Political Essays and Speeches of Two Decades*, trans. Helen Lowe-Porter and Agnes Meyer (Freeport, NY, 1969), pp. 83–7.

2 Ibid., pp. 114–42.

3 For a detailed description of Mann's years in Princeton, see Hans Rudolf Vaget, '"The Best of Worlds": Thomas Mann in Princeton', *Princeton University Library Chronicle*, LV (2013), pp. 9–37, a chapter of the forthcoming English version of Vaget's biography of the American years: *Thomas Mann, der Amerikaner: Leben und Werk im Amerikanischen Exil* (Frankfurt/Main, 2011).

4 The original German text carried the title 'Die Höhe des Augenblicks' (The High Moment) in *EK* V.

5 In English only in a pamphlet: Thomas Mann, *The Problem of Freedom* (New Brunswick, NJ, 1939).

6 *Common Sense* (New York, January 1940), pp. 11–14, under the misleading title 'In Defence of Wagner', cited in Hans Bürgin, *Bibliographie: Übersetzungen, Interviews* (Morsum/Sylt, 1992), p. 1003; as 'Zu Wagners Verteidigung' in *EK* V, 75–82.

7 See Ehrhard Bahr, *Weimar on the Pacific: German Exile Culture in Los Angeles and the Crisis of Modernism* (Berkeley, CA, 2007).

8 Hans Rudolf Vaget, *Thomas Mann: Kommentar zu sämtlichen Erzählungen* (Munich, 1984), pp. 252–6.

9 Woods gives Teje the name Tiy.

10 A short form of 'The War and the Future' is in Mann, *Order of the Day*, pp. 238–56. A much longer German draft is in *EK* V, 218–38, under the title 'Schicksal und Aufgabe'.

11   Letter of 29 May 1944, *BM* II, 366–8. See the letter to Ernst Reuter, 29 April 1944, *BM* II, 364–6; *LW*, 438–9.

8 *Doctor Faustus* and Discord with Germany

1   To Ida Herz, 24 August 1945: 'Grauen und eine neugierige Verbundenheit halten sich die Wage [*sic*]'. Thomas-Mann-Archive of the Swiss Federal Institute of Technology, Zurich.
2   Paul Deussen, *Erinnerungen an Friedrich Nietzsche* (Leipzig, 1901), p. 24.
3   Hans Rudolf Vaget, *Seelenzauber: Thomas Mann und die Musik* (Frankfurt/Main, 2006), pp. 38, 195, 225.
4   The chorus at the end of Beethoven's *Symphony No. 9* sings Friedrich Schiller's 'Ode to Joy' with the line: 'All men will be brothers.'
5   Hans Rudolf Vaget, 'Mann, Joyce, Wagner: The Question of Modernism in *Doctor Faustus*', and the response by David E. Wellbery, in *Thomas Mann's Doctor Faustus: A Novel at the Margin of Modernism*, ed. Herbert Lehnert and Peter C. Pfeiffer (Columbia, SC, 1991), pp. 167–97.

9 A Second Emigration: Tales of Forgiveness and Joy Emerge

1   The London edition appeared under the title *The Genesis of a Novel*, the American edition as *The Story of a Novel: The Genesis of Doctor Faustus*. Both editions were translated by Richard and Clara Winston.
2   The English translation was printed in college papers; it is not included in an essay volume.
3   Diary, 21 March 1950.
4   Only an abbreviated translation in *Harper's Magazine* (October 1950) is available.
5   Yvonne Schmidlin and Thomas Sprecher, eds, *Thomas Mann: Collegheft 1893–1895* (Frankfurt/Main, 2001), pp. 87, 97, 99, 103–4, 109–10, 112.
6   Edward R. Murrow, ed., *This I Believe*, broadcast, New York, 1952.

Select Bibliography

Works by Thomas Mann

Bürgin, Hans, ed., *Gesammelte Werke in Dreizehn Bänden* (Frankfurt/Main, 1960, 1974)

Detering, Heinrich, et al., eds, *Große kommentierte Frankfurter Ausgabe der Werke von Thomas Mann*, in progress (Frankfurt/Main, 2002–)

Dietzel, Ulrich, and Rosemarie Eggert, eds, *Heinrich Mann: Briefe an Ludwig Ewers, 1889–1913* (Berlin, 1980)

Jens, Inge, ed., *Tagebücher 1944 to 1. 4.1946* (Frankfurt/Main, 1986)

—, *Tagebücher 28.5.1946–31.12.1948* (Frankfurt/Main, 1989)

—, *Tagebücher, 1949–1950* (Frankfurt/Main, 1991)

—, *Tagebücher, 1951–1952* (Frankfurt/Main, 1993)

—, *Tagebücher 1953–1955* (Frankfurt/Main, 1995)

Kurzke, Hermann, and Stephan Stachorski, eds, *Essays*, 6 vols (Frankfurt/Main, 1993–7)

Mann, Erika, ed., *Thomas Mann: Briefe*, 3 vols (Frankfurt/Main, 1961–5)

Mann, Thomas, *The Problem of Freedom* (New Brunswick, NJ, 1939)

—, *Die Entstehung des Doktor Faustus: Roman eines Romans* (Amsterdam, 1949)

—, 'Germany Today: A Famous Exile's Impression of a Ruined, Vanquished Land and Unchanging People', *New York Times Magazine*, 25 September 1949

—, 'The Years of My Life', abbrev., *Harper's Magazine*, October 1950

—, *Thomas Mann's Addresses Delivered at the Library of Congress, 1942–1949* (Washington, DC, 1963)

Mendelssohn, Peter de, *Tagebücher, 1933–1934* (Frankfurt/Main, 1977)

—, *Tagebücher, 1935–1936* (Frankfurt/ Main, 1978)

—, *Thomas Mann: Tagebücher, 1918–1921* (Frankfurt/Main, 1979)

—, *Tagebücher, 1937–1939* (Frankfurt/Main, 1980)

—, *Tagebücher, 1940–1943* (Frankfurt/Main, 1982)

Potempa, Georg, ed., *Thomas Mann: Beteiligung an politschen Aufrufen und anderen kollektiven Publikationen* (Morsum/Sylt, 1988)

Schmidlin, Ivonne, and Thomas Sprecher, eds, *Thomas Mann: Collegheft 1893–1895* (Frankfurt/Main, 2001)

Wysling, Hans, and Marianne Fischer, eds, *Dichter über ihre Dichtungen*: *Thomas Mann*, 3 vols (Munich, 1975–81)

—, *Thomas Mann-Heinrich Mann: Briefwechsel 1900–1949* (Frankfurt/Main, 1995)

Wysling, Hans, and Yvonne Schmidlin, eds, *Thomas Mann Notizbücher*, 2 vols (Frankfurt/Main, 1991, 1992)

Works by Thomas Mann in English Translation

Buddenbrooks, trans. John E. Woods (New York, 1993)

Confessions of Felix Krull, Confidence Man: Memoirs, Part 1, trans. Denver Lindley (London, 1977)

'Death in Venice' and other Stories by Thomas Mann, trans. David Luke (New York, 1988)

Death in Venice and other Tales, trans. Joachim Neugroschel (New York, 1998)

Doktor Faustus, trans. John E. Woods (New York, 1997)

Essays of Three Decades, trans. Helen Lowe-Porter (New York, 1947)

Joseph and his Brothers, trans. John E. Woods (New York, 2005)

Last Essays, trans. Tania Stern and James Stern (New York, 1959)

Letters of Heinrich and Thomas Mann, 1900–1949, ed. Hans Wysling, trans. Don Renau (Berkeley, CA, 1998)

Letters of Thomas Mann, ed. and trans. Clara and Richard Winston (New York, 1971)

Lotte in Weimar: The Beloved Returns, trans. Helen Lowe-Porter (Berkeley, CA, 1990)

Order of the Day: Political Essays and Speeches of Two Decades, trans. Helen Lowe-Porter and Agnes Meyer (Freeport, NY, 1969) [Meyer translated only pp. 114–42]

Postmasters and Other Papers: Thomas Mann, trans. Helen Lowe-Porter
(Freeport, NY, 1968)
Reflections of a Nonpolitial Man: Thomas Mann, trans. Walter D. Morris
(New York, 1983)
Royal Highness, trans. with a new Preface by A. Cecil Curtis, intro. Alan Sica
(Berkeley, CA, 1992)
Stories of a Lifetime, 2 vols, trans Helen Lowe-Porter and Willard R. Trask
(New York, 1970) [Trask translated 'The Black Swan', vol. II, pp. 348–411]
The Genesis of a Novel, ed. and trans. Clara and Richard Winston
(London, 1961)
The Holy Sinner, trans. Helen Lowe-Porter (New York, 1951)
The Magic Mountain: A Novel, trans. John E. Woods (New York, 1995)
The Story of a Novel: The Genesis of Doctor Faustus, ed. and trans.
Clara and Richard Winston (New York, 1961)
This I Believe, broadcast, ed. Edward R. Murrow (New York, 1952)

Secondary Literature and Context

Bahr, Ehrhard, *Thomas Mann, Der Tod in Venedig, Erläuterungen und
Documente* (Stuttgart, 2005)
—, *Weimar on the Pacific: German Exile Culture in Los Angeles and the Crisis of
Modernism* (Berkeley, CA, 2007)
Bin Gorion, Micha Joseph (Micha Joseph Berdyczewski), *Die Sagen der
Juden* (Frankfurt/Main, 1919)
Böhm, Karl Werner, *Zwischen Selbstzucht und Verlangen: Thomas Mann und
das Stigma Homosexualität* (Würzburg, 1991)
Brainin, S. N., trans., Jacob Wassermann, *My Life as German and Jew*
(New York, 1933)
Burckhardt, Jacob, *The Civilization of the Renaissance in Italy*, 15th edn
(London, 1929)
Deussen, Paul, *Erinnerungen an Friedrich Nietzsche* (Leipzig, 1901)
Dierks, Manfred, 'Thomas Mann's Late Politics', in *A Companion of
the Works of Thomas Mann*, ed. Herbert Lehnert and Eva Wessell
(Rochester, NY, 2004), pp. 203–19
—, *Thomas Manns Geisterbaron: Leben und Werk von Schrenck-Notzing*
(Gießen, 2012)

Eicken, Friedrich, *Geschichte und System der mittelalterlichen Weltanschauung*
(Stuttgart, 1887)

Häberlin, Karl Ludwig (H.E.R. Belani), *Goethe und sein Liebeleben* [*sic*]:
Historischer Novellenkreis, vol. II (Leipzig, 1866)

Hahn, Manfred, Anne Flierl and Wolfgang Klein, eds, *Heinrich Mann,*
Essays und Publizistic: Kritische Gesamtausgabe, vol. II (Bielefeld, 2012)

Heller, Erich, *The Ironic German: A Study of Thomas Mann* (Boston, MA, 1958)

Jens, Walter, and Inge Jens, *Frau Thomas Mann: Das Leben der Katharina*
Pringsheim (Reinbek, 2003)

Jeremias, Alfred, *Das alte Testament im Lichte des Alten Orients* (Leipzig, 1904)

Landauer, Gustav, *For Socialism*, trans. David J. Parent
(Saint Louis, MO, 1978)

Mann, Heinrich, *Ein Zeitalter wird besichtigt* (Berlin, 1973)

—, *Novellen. Zweiter Band* (Berlin, 1978)

—, *Briefe an Ludwig Ewers, 1889–1913*, trans. Ulrich Dietzel and Rosemarie
Eggert (Berlin, 1980)

Mann, Katia, *Meine ungeschriebenen Memoiren*, ed. Elisabeth Plessen and
Michael Mann (Frankfurt/Main, 1974)

Marcus, Judith, *Georg Lukács and Thomas Mann: A Study in the Sociology*
of Literature (Amherst, MA, 1987)

Muschg, Walter, *Tragische Literaturgeschichte* (Bern, 1948)

Nietzsche, Friederich, *Sämtliche: Werke. Kritische Studienausgabe* (KSA),
15 vols, ed. Giorgio Colli and Mazzino Montinari (Munich, 1988)

Pütz, Peter, 'Joseph and his Brothers', in *A Companion to the Works of*
Thomas Mann, ed. Herbert Lehnert and Eva Wessell (Rochester,
NY, 2004), pp. 159–79

Reed, Terence James, *Thomas Mann: The Uses of Tradition*, 2nd edn
(Oxford, 1996)

Saine, Thomas P., 'Passion and Aggression: The Meaning of Werther's
Last Letter', *Orbis Litterarum*, XXXV (1980), pp. 327–56

Shookman, Ellis, *Thomas Mann's Death in Venice: A Novella and Its*
Critics (Rochester, NY, 2003)

Siefken, Hinrich, 'Lotte in Weimar – "Contactnahme" and Thomas Mann's
Novel about Goethe', *Trivium*, XIII (1978), pp. 38–52

—, 'Thomas Mann's Novel "Lotte in Weimar" – a "Lustspiel"?'
Oxford German Studies, XI (1980), pp. 103–22

—, *Thomas Mann: 'Ideal der Deutschheit'* (Munich, 1981)

Stein, Peter, ed., *Heinrich Man: Essays und Publizistik: Kritische Gesamtausgabe*, vol. I (Bielefeld, 2013)

Theilhaber, Felix, *Goethe: Sexus und Eros* (Berlin, 1929)

Vaget, Hans Rudolf, 'Thomas Mann und Theodor Fontane: Eine rezeptionsästhetische Studie zu "Der kleine Herr Friedemann"', *Modern Language Notes*, XC (1975), pp. 448–71

—, *Thomas Mann, Kommentar zu sämtlichen Erzählungen* (Munich, 1984)

—, 'Mann, Joyce, Wagner: The Question of Modernism in *Doctor Faustus*', in *Thomas Mann's Doctor Faustus: A Novel at the Margin of Modernism*, ed. Herbert Lehnert and Peter C. Pfeiffer, with a response by David E. Wellbery (Columbia, SC, 1991), pp. 167–97

—, *Seelenzauber: Thomas Mann und die Musik* (Frankfurt/Main, 2006)

—, '"The Best of Worlds": Thomas Mann in Princeton', *Princeton University Library Chronicle*, vol. LV (2013), pp. 9–37

Villari, Pasquale, *Life and Times of Girolamo Savonarola* (New York, 1909)

Yisrael, Mimekor, *Classical Jewish Folktale*s (Bloomington, IL, 1976)

Acknowledgements

We are grateful for the help we received with the completion of this manuscript from the following organizations and their associates: the University of California, Irvine, with its Interlibrary Loan facility; Dr Katrin Bedenig and her staff, especially Rolf Bolt, at the Thomas-Mann-Archive of the Swiss Federal Institute of Technology in Zurich, which supplied the majority of our illustrations; Britta Dittmann for her help with images at the Buddenbrookhaus Museum in Lübeck, and Elke Krüger at the photo archive at the Sankt Annen Museum there; Frank Schmitter at the Monacensia literary archive of the Stadtbibliothek Munich; and Roland Spar and Doris Mall at the S. Fischer Verlag in Frankfurt/Main. We thank Nicolas Jacobs who was always ready to give advice in tight language spots. A special thank you must go to the friendly and helpful staff at Reaktion, especially Amy Salter and Harry Gilonis.

Photo Acknowledgements

The author and publishers wish to express their thanks to the below sources of illustrative material and/or permission to reproduce it.

Reproduced courtesy the Buddenbrookhaus, Lübeck: pp. 19, 34; photos courtesy the Buddenbrookhaus, Lübeck (© S. Fischer Verlag, Frankfurt am Main): pp. 70, 148; photos © der Hansestadt Lübeck, reproduced by kind permission: pp. 13, 152; photo Hans Kripganz (reproduced courtesy the Buddenbrookhaus, Lübeck): p. 155; Library of Congress, Washington, DC (Prints and Photographs Division – Carl Van Vechten Collection): p. 9; photo Stadtbibliothek München: p. 118; reproduced by kind permission of the Thomas-Mann-Archiv, Zürich: pp. 16, 17, 23, 43, 46, 56, 57, 62, 67, 75, 78, 79, 80, 84, 85, 86, 87, 89, 91, 96, 103, 113.